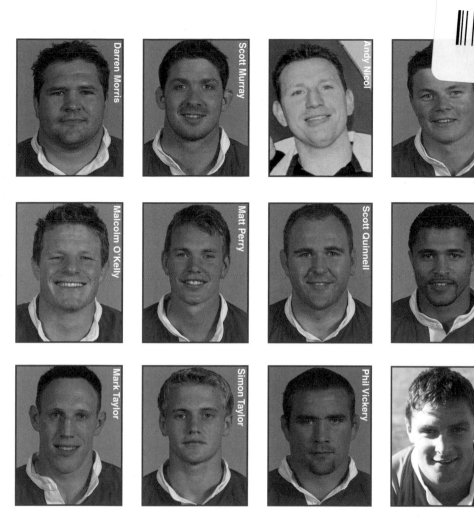

THE OFFICIAL BOOK OF THE
Lions Tour to Australia 2001

WOUNDED PRIDE

Mick Cleary

Foreword by
WILLIE JOHN McBRIDE

Reflections on the tour from
**Graham Henry,
Michael Lynagh and Lawrence Dallaglio**

Photographs by
Allsport

MAINSTREAM
PUBLISHING

First published in Great Britain in 2001 by
MAINSTREAM PUBLISHING COMPANY (EDINBURGH) LTD
7 Albany Street
Edinburgh EH1 3UG

ISBN 1 84018 518 X

A catalogue record for this book is available from the British Library

Produced by Lennard Books
A division of Lennard Associates Limited
Mackerye End, Harpenden, Herts, AL5 5DR

Production Editor: Chris Marshall
Text and cover design: Paul Cooper Design

Printed and bound in Great Britain by
Butler & Tanner, Frome and London

ACKNOWLEDGEMENTS

The publishers would like to thank Dave Rogers and Nick Wilson of Allsport
and all other members of the Allsport team that provided such an excellent photographic coverage
of the Lions tour - Scott Barbour, Darrin Braybrook, Chris McGrath, Adam Pretty and Matt Turner.
Thanks also to Neil Loft and Justin Davies in the Allsport London office for their editorial support,
and to Amy Cracknell for her keyboard skills

**A SPECIAL THANK YOU TO
SINGAPORE AIRLINES
FOR TRANSPORTING THE LIONS PARTY
IN GREAT COMFORT
TO AND FROM AUSTRALIA**

Contents

BEWARE

CHAMPIONING THE LIONS IN AUSTRALIA.

ZURIC

Foreword by SANDY LEITCH

Chief Executive, Zurich Financial Services UKISA

To be so closely involved with the 2001 Lions tour – one of sport's greatest events – was an immense privilege for Zurich. Our sponsorship of the Lions was, in many ways, a natural extension of our already deep-rooted association with rugby union formed largely through our sponsorship of the Zurich Premiership and Zurich Championship.

Zurich is a global leader in providing financial protection and investment solutions. We have a major presence in the UK through household names such as Allied Dunbar, Threadneedle and Eagle Star, but the Zurich name is, at present, still relatively unknown.

Sponsorship of the Lions has helped to increase our profile in the UK and on a new international stage. We were also delighted to be a part of Sky Sports coverage of the tour appealing to the many sports fans that tuned in at home to follow the team's fortunes.

Despite the fierce and intense battles on the field, rugby is a game of congregation – not segregation. There could have been no better demonstration of that than to witness the magnificent support in Australia. Thousands of English, Irish, Scottish and Welsh fans combined to form a sea of red and stun the Wallabies as

they rolled into each new venue, with the night at the Gabba set to live long in the memory.

Zurich's sponsorship of rugby at all levels is a positive endorsement of the growth we anticipate and the success we want. However, our support and sponsorship of rugby is more than banners and financial backing. We want to be involved — in the thick of the action and close to the emotion. We aim to be a valued and responsible partner to this great sport.

Rugby union is a passionate, thrilling game where virtues, such as teamwork, discipline, honesty, skill and resourcefulness, are found in abundance. It is that passion that we at Zurich want to nurture. We believe in this game and we aim to be one of its most important supporters.

As our focus once again returns to the domestic field, we look forward to seeing the Zurich Premiership promoting these values and nurturing more talent to take on the mighty All Blacks in 2005.

Sandy Leitch

Sandy Leitch with Jeremy Guscott and Lawrence Dallaglio at the Zurich Golf Day at Hope Island Resort, near Brisbane.

What goes on tour now goes on TV.

Get **ntl digitalplus,** the digital TV service from **ntl,** and you'll not just have access to all the games in Australia
get Lions TV, bringing you stats, facts and exclusive behind-the-scenes footage throughout the tour. For more in

SUPPORTERS OF THE 2001 LIONS

DOWN UNDER

Caffrey's - Official Beer of the 2001 Lions

 Official Beer of the 2001 Lions

Introduction by WILLIE JOHN McBRIDE

Successful Lions tours depend on all sorts of things, but if you have good management, a top-class coaching team and a group of 20 outstanding players in a well-balanced squad of over 30 players the main ingredients are in place for a winning series.

What you do not want is a six-week trip to Australia where the Test side is ravaged by injuries to key players and at least half of the likely Test team are unavailable for selection for the final match of the tour with the series delicately balanced at one Test all. Sadly that is what happened to the 2001 Lions and they had to go into the third Test without a host of players who would have been first-choice selections.

It underlined for me how desperately unlucky the 2001 Lions were compared to my last tour as a Lions player in 1974. We won the first three Tests in South Africa to win the series and used just 16 players for all three of those Tests. The one change we did make was not because of injury but a selection decision to put Andy Irvine on the right wing in place of Billy Steele.

Graham Henry and Martin Johnson had no such luck in 2001. It must have been soul-destroying for them. Indeed in the week before the final Test, because of injury problems the Test team were never able to train together. After the Test in Melbourne five of the players were unfit to train on the Sunday, Monday, Tuesday and Wednesday leading up to the decisive Sydney Test. Scott Quinnell nursed his leg injury the whole week without training, Neil Back, Jonny Wilkinson, Brian O'Driscoll and Rob Henderson managed one session each at the end of the week and Austin Healey, who had been able to train, then dropped out of the side on the Saturday morning in Sydney with a back spasm.

This was not the ideal build-up for such an important match. After all, the Lions were playing the best team in the world. Australia in July 2001 were the world champions, the Tri-Nations champions, the holders of the Bledisloe Cup (v New Zealand), the Mandela Cup (v South Africa), the Hopetoun Cup (v Scotland) and the Lansdowne Cup (v Ireland).

It speaks volumes for Martin Johnson and his Lions side that they were level with Australia going into the final 20 minutes of the game. Unfortunately for all their earlier heroics they had failed to score a single point in the last 20 minutes of the first or second Tests, and they failed to do so again in the third.

The record books will show it was a losing series, but, if nothing else, the Lions lost to a great Australian side, brilliantly led by John Eales and coached by Rod Macqueen. The record books won't show the wonderful, fanatical following of 25,000 British and Irish supporters who made the Test series so special and such a spectacle as they turned the Gabba in Brisbane, the Colonial Stadium in Melbourne, and Stadium Australia in Sydney into a sea of red jerseys.

I enjoyed my three weeks 'down under' enormously, even though we lost the series. The first Test produced one of the very best Lions performances in the last 40 years. The Wallabies were overwhelmed and made to look decidedly second best. The forwards were magnificent and the backs had their best match of the tour. It was superb 15-man attacking rugby at its very best and a huge credit to the four home unions.

The first half in Melbourne was almost as good, and the tragedy was that the Lions led by just 11-6 at half-time. They created a handful of great scoring opportunities in a prolonged period on the attack, but a couple of wrong options and some desperate Wallaby defence thwarted them. They could have been 20 points clear at half-time and should have won the second Test.

At 23-23 in Sydney they could still have won the third Test, but in the end the better team on the day took the game, and the Wallabies won a series against the Lions for the first time.

The good news is that Lions rugby once again captured the imagination of the whole rugby world, and a huge global audience enjoyed a really great Test series. There is nothing quite as exciting and dramatic as a Lions tour, with the possible exception of a World Cup.

I am already looking forward to two more visits to Australia in the next four years. Roll on the World Cup in Australia and New Zealand in 2003 and the Lions tour to New Zealand in 2005. Northern hemisphere rugby is in pretty good shape.

Willie John McBride.

Lion King

OFFICIAL VEHICLE SUPPLIER TO THE 2001 LIONS

The 2001 Lions Tour sees Britain and Ireland's strongest, toughest and most capable competing on a global level. It demands guts, spirit, stamina and a sense of purpose beyond the everyday.

And a world beating team requires a world-beating vehicle. Which is why the Lions will be taking the best 4x4 by far to Australia with them - Range Rover, king of the off-road. So if you feel like joining them, call 0800 110 110 for an information pack.

official vehicle supplier

THE BEST 4x4xFAR

1. **Preparation**

The media receive the announcement of the Lions party to Australia at the Crowne Plaza, Heathrow, on 25 April 2001.

Flight No. TG 995 from Bangkok to Perth had just been called. We got up to go. Lee Smith looked across forlornly to where we were gathering our bags. 'Wish I was going to where you fellows are headed,' he said.

Smith is the Game Development Manager for the International Board. He's done a bit in his time, travelling the world to spread the word. He himself was in transit from Heathrow, where our paths had crossed, and was now off to Sri Lanka, then returning to Thailand before going to New Zealand. It wasn't the worst route in the world. But he was right. There was only one place to go, only one game on planet rugby – and that was down in Australia. The British and Irish Lions had stirred from their four-yearly hibernation and were headed south. So were we.

The bug had bitten everyone. In the two months leading up to departure in early June all manner of people had mentioned that they too were bound for Australia or knew someone who

was – my doctor's cousin, the brother of TV chef Ainsley Harriott, the list was endless with some 10,000 fans expected to hit Australia. Only the Lions can do this. Only the Lions can draw a bigger travelling band of supporters than pitched up for the Sydney Olympics nine months earlier. Only the Lions have the allure and the uniqueness to do this.

The Lions are the perfect mix of the old and the new, of romance and tradition, of streamlined professionalism gathered under the banner of ancient brotherhood. They are a different act, a radical change of set-up from the regular grind. They are both exotic yet homely, a rich blend of new faces, unlikely combinations and burgeoning friendships. In the long-drawn-out calendar of international rugby, the Lions present a fresh challenge for themselves and their opponents. The Australian public keenly awaited their arrival, having grown jaded by the cycle of Super-12 and Tri-Nations, with essentially the same players drawn from the three countries doing their annual trawl round the southern hemisphere.

The four home unions, by nature conservative, were to be applauded for their…er…conservatism. They alone of all modern administrators had recognised that the curse of modern rugby lay in the pile-up of fixtures and tournaments. That way was not to be their way. For them, less is actually more. The value of the Lions lies in their rarity. They are treasured and revered because the love affair is so brief – two months every four years. As a result the relationship is always passionate and never stale. There is no time to fall out, to discover unseemly habits or for life to become mundane and predictable. Take your eye off the ball for a second and you've missed the treat.

The home unions have resisted the call – and you can bet that their phone has been hot at various times with entrepreneurs looking to cash in – to allow the Lions to play more often or even to play one-off games in Britain or Ireland. Perish the thought. The home unions stuck with tradition. They invested their modernist tendencies, such as they were, in ensuring that the 2001 Lions had the best possible support systems in place, the best facilities, the best back-up, the best preparations. It didn't come cheap – some £3 million – but it was money well spent.

There was talk when the game turned professional in 1995 that the Lions might suffer. That's all that thought ever was – talk. The concept never got past the tittle-tattle stage. The Lions are a stronger brand than ever, in all senses. They drew a portfolio of blue chip sponsors to the 2001 tour – ntl, Zurich, adidas, Caffrey's, Land Rover. They are the only combined sporting team from the four countries, cutting across frontiers and prejudices.

In many ways the Lions are a contradiction, living proof that the enduring appeal of sport has little to do with logic and everything to do with emotion. How else to explain how the players and fans from the four disparate countries, united by politics yet divided by politics, who speak one tongue apart from the fiercely partisan pockets where Welsh and Gaelic languages are spoken, can

thrive on those ancient enmities for four years and then bury them in the blink of an eye?

How can the Six Nations Championship flourish by playing the nationalist card for all it is worth, by elevating the deep national rivalries, by – let's get this one out in the open – the three others all ganging up to hate England, and for all that to be then immediately buried when the Lions bugle call to arms is sounded every four years? Mad. Quite mad. And long may madness reign!

The old line – and a damn good one it was too – that Lions tours are a cross between a medieval crusade and a school outing may no longer hold true. The fact is that the tours are much more condensed, much more concentrated on the playing out on the pitch and not playing away from home, whatever that might entail. Gone is the sense of rollicking fun that attached itself to the rambling tours of old, which set off in early May and were still at it three months later. The modern game does not allow for such indulgences.

But that does not mean that the Lions have lost something. They have not. They have simply redefined themselves and done it quite splendidly. They may have lost some of their sepia-tinted mystique, that feeling of a bunch of sporting marauders doing their thing in distant lands, news of which was relayed only through newspaper reports. The tours were only ever covered by a handful of journalists, men such as Vivian Jenkins and Terry O'Connor, whose missives from foreign fields would be pored over the next morning as they winged in from faraway parts. That, too, has all changed. Over 100 media people turned up for the announcement of the squad. Many more pitched up in Australia – with their pens, their digital cameras, their internet feeds, their TV cameras, their websites, their DVDs and all manner of other electronic trappings. The Lions are no longer a well-kept secret. Everyone wants a slice of the action. Especially the players.

But first they had to get the trip. 'There are two phases to a Lions selection,' says England and Wasps back-row forward Lawrence Dallaglio. 'First you've got to make the plane. Then it starts all over again as you try to make the Test team.' And who would do the picking for the 2001 British and Irish

Lions? Step forward Donal Lenihan, appointed manager by the home unions committee from a shortlist including Roger Uttley and Derek Quinnell, Lions themselves in the 1970s and steeped in the Lions traditions. So too was Lenihan. He had recent experience of playing and of managing. He emerged as the midweek captain during the 1989 Lions tour to Australia, the Irish lock seeing the value of keeping the group together once players like himself realised that a Test spot was not to be theirs.

Lenihan had also had a stint as manager of the Irish national side. The role was no longer that of a glorified frontman, the official stooge for all manner of civic functions. In the professional era the manager was a key man, the one who had to put in place the infrastructure as well as the one who had to know his way down the page to the bottom line. The playing contract was an important piece of literature. Of course, every single player in the four home countries would crawl across broken glass to be chosen for the Lions. But the terms and the conditions have to be fair. On both sides. It is not simply a case of how much. It is also a case of bonus incentives, of obligations to sponsors, of intellectual property rights – one of the bugbears that triggered the 24-hour strike by England players just prior to the autumn international against Argentina. The paperwork all had to be sound and in proper order. It was.

Lenihan was appointed in January 2000. He had a primary duty to perform – to get a coach. His brief was simple. He wanted the best man for the job. There was one name at the top of his list – Ian McGeechan; no surprise, given that Geech was top of nearly everyone's list. He had done the job three times already, winning twice, in Australia in 1989 and then in South Africa in 1997. His only failure was in 1993 in New Zealand, and it was of the glorious kind (or the larcenous kind to be more accurate, with a desperately dodgy refereeing decision by Australian Brian Kinsey robbing the Lions of victory in the last minute of the first Test.)

Lenihan wanted Geech. Geech cherished the Lions. He knew and understood what made a Lions player tick, what made a Lions tour come together, better than anyone on the planet. He knew how

much work it would take. The foundations for that stunning 1997 victory over the Springboks had been laid a year earlier when McGeechan had spent three weeks tracking the All Blacks through South Africa, watching their every move, plotting and scheming every step of the way. He was taken into the All Blacks inner sanctum by coach John Hart and captain Sean Fitzpatrick, a generous gesture and one that Geech used to good effect. He insisted that his Lions had to be self-sufficient in every sense, bussing their scrum machine around the country and enlarging the squad to 35 players in order to provide rest for key men in midweek.

Geech created the template. But it was not to be McGeechan this time. Despite several visits from Lenihan and several phone calls from home unions chairman Syd Millar, McGeechan went with his head and not with his heart. His conscience told him that he had too much work to do in his new role with Scotland. 'I could not commit fully to the Lions,' said McGeechan. 'And if you can't commit fully, better not to commit at all. I did not want to fall between two stools and fail both sides.'

Lenihan already had another name in mind, that of Graham Henry, a New Zealander by birth and a coach of the first order by trade. Henry, a former headmaster at Kelston Boys High in Auckland, had made his name when coaching the provincial side in that city. Auckland won Super-12 titles under Henry in 1996 and 1997, finishing runners-up to the Canterbury Crusaders the following year. Wales pounced in 1998 to help salvage their plummeting reputation on the world scene. Ten straight wins, including their first ever victory over the Springboks in 1999, was not a bad effort. Henry had pedigree, and that was all that interested Lenihan. He made the call. Henry accepted and was named Lions coach in June 2000. The fact that he was the first foreigner to coach the Lions did not sit well with everyone. Former Lions Roger Uttley and John Jeffrey weighed in with complaints, so too England manager Clive Woodward.

Lenihan took the criticism and backed his man. 'Of course I would have preferred someone from the home countries and that's why I went for Geech,' he said. 'But Graham Henry was by far the best candidate after that. That has been my only criterion, for management and for players. Nationality does not enter into the equation on any count.' By the end of the month another name had been added to the selection panel, that of Andy Robinson, the former Bath and England flanker who had just taken over as coach with England alongside Woodward. He too was a Lion, having played in Lenihan's midweek side through the 1989 tour.

Twelve months to go and already the tour was taking shape. By the end of that summer, the first names were being pencilled in. The clock was ticking. It was the only thing that was making a noise when the three men – Lenihan, Henry and Robinson – met formally for the first time against the charming, sleepy backdrop of Clonakilty, a fishing village in Cork. They talked names and they talked strategy. The first significant pulse of the 2001 Lions was beating strongly.

The management of (l to r) Andy Robinson, Graham Henry and Donal Lenihan at the Arms Park, Cardiff, in October 2000.

They drew up criteria for players, who were divided into three groups – the definites, the possibles and the wide outsiders to keep an eye on. 'The man in the street could have given you 15 names at that stage that we'd all have agreed on,' said Lenihan. 'We were never too bothered about the top boys through the year, aside from checking that they were alive.'

Lenihan drew in others to the Lions circle. Five selectors were chosen to help the management with their deliberations – John Rutherford and Ian Lawrie from Scotland, Simon Halliday from England, Derek Quinnell from Wales and John O'Driscoll from Ireland – a cross section of interests and backgrounds.

By the time Lenihan stood before the assembled media throng in the Guggenheim Room at the Crowne Plaza Hotel at Heathrow, the selectors had watched some 200 matches between them. They had met several times through the season to compare notes and trade information. Each time, the

list was whittled down, names were added, one or two were scored out. In early spring a long list of 67 names was released. It was purely a bureaucratic formality, prompted by a need to check availability and sort out insurance matters. It was of no lasting significance. In 1997 five players not on the initial long list made it into the final group. So, perhaps not too much should have been read into the list..

At a rough guess only about half a kilometre of newspaper column inches was eventually clocked up on the subject. Everything was read into the list, every conspiracy theory explored, every snub drummed up. The great fun of Lions tours is the sense of anticipation involved. The taproom debaters were in their element. And the media were quite happy to trawl those pub taprooms to gauge reaction. Professional duty, you understand.

There was no place for Scotland captain, scrum half Andy Nicol. No place either for ex-rugby league star Jason Robinson, who had made an instant impact when called up unexpectedly by England. There was no indication either at that stage who might be chosen to lead the Lions into battle. Martin Johnson again? Ireland's great warrior Keith Wood? Lawrence Dallaglio? Matt Dawson? David Young? The names tripped off the tongue. The appetite was being teased.

And then came foot-and-mouth. Just when it seemed that all was moving smoothly towards an announcement on 12 April, four days after the scheduled end of the Six Nations Championship, the English countryside erupted. Foot-and-mouth ravaged farms and caused panic among politicians. Sporting bodies fell into line. Ireland, so heavily reliant on the farming industry, adopted a policy of zero tolerance. Three championship games were postponed – the matches in Cardiff and Edinburgh and the home game against England. The tournament was a damp squib. England captured hearts and minds with their invigorating rugby. But there was no title to be captured.

There was to be no final scrutiny either for the selectors. They had 30 names more or less set in stone. All the real head-scratching involved the final seven names. The selectors needed more time to see the fringe candidates put to the test. The Heineken Cup semi-finals were not until late April.

Selector on selector as John Rutherford of Scotland tackles England's Simon Halliday at Twickenham in 1987.

The squad announcement was delayed until those games – Munster against Stade Français, Leicester against Gloucester – had taken place. Wednesday 25 April was the rearranged D-day. 'It was an inconvenience but no more than that,' said Lenihan. 'If your selection is coming down to how guys do in just one or two matches, then there's something wrong with your selection process. You know the type of guys you are looking for. You want great players with a willingness to be positive and responsible in a Lions context.'

And what was the overriding criterion, the one element that would make all the difference? 'For every single player we pick there is one thought at the back of our minds. The series is tied at 1-1 and it's the last 15 minutes of the third Test. Can he take the pressure?' said Lenihan.

On the stroke of 11 a.m., as the jets roared overhead at Heathrow Airport, Lenihan read out the 37 names of those that he and his selectors felt could take the pressure. A few nods of approval among the media throng, then a few murmurs and the occasional raised eyebrow.

'Johnson, Wood, Wilkinson, Howley…'

No surprise there.

'Martyn Williams, Malcolm O'Kelly…'

Hmm. Yeah. OK. Fine. Good performers. But who has missed out as a result? Here it comes.

'Rob Henderson, Ronan O'Gara, Simon Taylor…'

A shuffle of notes. Where's Scott Gibbs? Where's Gregor Townsend? Not there. Two men who had helped take the Lions to victory in South Africa four years earlier passed over for this trip? Gibbs, whose jabbing finger in the huddle before the critical second Test in Durban captured the mood of defiance of that squad, had not done enough after a patchy season. Townsend, a mercurial figure but one whose shimmying talent had kept the

Jeremy Davidson (right) got the nod, but there was no place for his mercurial Castres clubmate Gregor Townsend (centre).

Springboks guessing (and kept his own team-mates guessing too), had not made the cut. The selectors had made a trip to Paris to see him play a French championship match for his club, Castres, against Stade Français. Townsend's score in the final minutes helped his side steal away with victory. It was not enough to help him steal away with Lions selection. His Castres clubmate, Ireland lock Jeremy Davidson, got all the good news that was winging its way down into southern France that day.

Bold decisions. But bold is what the Lions are all about. And they don't come much bigger and bolder than Martin Johnson, who became the first man to ever lead the Lions twice. The squad was announced on Wednesday. Johnson got the call on Monday evening at home. When the phone rang, he broke off from talking to his wife, Kay. A little later he came back into the living room and sat down. Ten minutes after that his wife asked him who had been on the phone. 'Donal Lenihan,' said Johnno, playing the nonplussed card for all it was worth. It might not suit the beetle-browed exterior

to describe him as tickled pink, but pink and tickled is what he was.

More bold decisions – Jason Robinson. The long list had stretched a bit further. Robinson had done enough in his three England appearances from the bench to convince the men that mattered that he was made of the right stuff, the last 15 minutes stuff. And all that after just 22 games of union since joining Sale from Wigan in October. It was the most significant conversion of the season. Robinson had been living life on the fast track.

'Jason is still on the upward part of the graph as far as his learning goes,' said Henry. The gradient was about to become Himalayan. There were other marginal calls – Robin McBryde at hooker instead of Scotland's Gordon Bulloch; David Young on the tight-head over the younger Englishman Julian White, although Young's solid citizenship and good humour tipped the balance, as well as his potential leadership qualities for the midweek side.

In many households and on many training grounds around the four countries, players were reaching for the Ceefax button. There was joy and disappointment in equal measure. No Kyran Bracken, Joe Worsley or Martin Corry from England. No Denis Hickie or John Hayes from Ireland. No Budge Pountney from Scotland.

There was one Scot who was leaping through hoops – No. 8 Simon Taylor, a 21-year-old law student at Edinburgh University. And who he? Let's ask the management. What did you write down about him at that first selection meeting down in Clonakilty? 'I think it would be fair to say that none of us had ever heard of him,' said Lenihan. 'But that's the beauty of a Lions year. Players can come from nowhere to mount a challenge.'

Taylor himself must have been on tenterhooks. Or not. He was tracked down by the Scottish Rugby Union, who broke the news to him. 'I am in complete shock,' said Taylor when the press phone calls started flooding through. 'My ambition was to challenge for the 2005 tour. It never occurred to me that I might be in the frame for this one.'

Taylor, who had shown well for the Scotland Under 21 side at the SANZAR tournament the previous summer, had made his full debut against the USA in the autumn. Next up were the

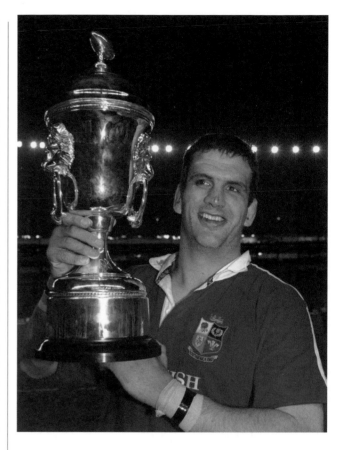

Martin Johnson, seen here after the victorious 1997 series, became the first player ever to captain two Lions tours.

Wallabies. After five minutes, Taylor broke a bone in his hand; 75 minutes later he trotted down the tunnel at the final whistle. The Lions like players who can take a bit of pain in their stride. 'We had a gut feeling about him,' said Lenihan. The innards did not tell a lie.

There were other selections that tiptoed along the fine line. England wing Dan Luger had been injured in the early stages of the game against Wales, the opening match of the Six Nations. He had damaged a nerve in his neck and had not touched a ball in anger since. He was back in full training with his club, Saracens, and had been given a clean bill of health by his own physiotherapist, Kevin Lidlow, a few days earlier. But he hadn't played a game. The Lions went bold again. Luger got the nod.

Warrior-turned-Shark Jason Robinson missed the long list but hit the shortlist after three replacement appearances for England.

'I did have doubts in my own mind,' said Luger. 'And in the minds of some doctors. One of them asked me if I did anything else for a living when I went to see him in February. He figured that I wouldn't be playing rugby for some time. The best case scenario was three months. And that really was best case. That left me a couple of weeks outside selection. The foot-and-mouth delay probably helped my case. I was thrilled to hear the news. We'd been training at Southgate and didn't come off until after the squad had been announced. Our fly half, Duncan McRae, told me that I'd made it. I then had to check for myself in case it was a wind-up.' Cruel if it had been. Not even the most spiteful of blokes would do that. There is a time and a place for wind-ups. This was not one of them.

Listen to Scott Gibbs, a man who'd been with the Lions to New Zealand in 1993 and South Africa in 1997, a man who'd won over that most

hardbitten, begrudging bunch, rugby league diehards, with his play for St Helens, a man who had seen success at all levels and experienced sporting life to the full. 'The disappointment will take a long time to get over,' said the 30-year-old Swansea captain who has won 53 caps for Wales. 'April has been the cruellest month. I had hoped that my experience with the Lions would count for something, but it is not up to me to quarrel with my selection. Another day dawns and no one else knows what awaits.'

Gibbs joined the fingers-crossed category of those who might be on standby should an injury befall someone in their position. It's the last clutch of the straw, but it is one all those players were snatching at. An average of six players are forced to return early from Lions trips. It's an unforgiving sporting landscape.

It was an impressive morning in the grey surrounds of a Heathrow Airport hotel. Never mind the drab backdrop. It was a theatrical day, well-staged by the Lions PR people at Octagon. There is no need for glitz and glamour on these occasions. There is a simple equation at work in these matters. The more glitz and razzamatazz that surrounds a sporting event, the less likely it is to have real and lasting quality. The true drama is in the news itself, not the packaging.

There was a buzz in the air as we waited for the 37 names, and then silence fell as Syd Millar opened proceedings, and not just because we are a polite lot (which we aren't) or because Millar is a giant of a man who has tamed many a fearsome opponent in his time (which he has). No, the reading of the names is a ritual, a delicious moment in the lifespan of any touring side. 'And to think that we used to do this before a couple of scribes along a corridor at the East India Club,' said Millar.

Other things have changed too. There used to be no end of political horse-trading in the committee rooms as each union's representative fought his corner. Each and every tour up to 1997 had seen at least two players bumped on political grounds, two players included because of where they were born not how they were playing. It happened to England tight-head Jeff Probyn as recently as 1993. It did not happen this time.

The squad had the air of one that was properly and rationally selected, regardless of nationality. There were gripes as to who should have gone – Gibbs and Townsend, perhaps – but there could be no accusations levelled that it had been through bias and not reason. 'There was no consideration given to nationality,' said the man whose nationality had stirred a little hornet's nest.

Henry and Lenihan had also finalised the management team. Phil Larder was to come along as defence coach, probably the most important element of all when piecing together a new side. Larder, a former Great Britain rugby league coach, has amply demonstrated the importance of his skills with England and Leicester, the meanest defensive operators of all.

Dave Alred was eventually signed up to oversee kicking duties, a not inconsiderable job given that Test matches have a habit of being decided by the width of a post. Steve Black, a Geordie of many parts and a human being of infectious enthusiasm, was to be fitness coach, not to mention wet nurse,

large shoulder to cry on, top bloke, late night companion, early morning training partner, an all-round prop to every need of every member of the squad. On Lions tours, at the end of a gruelling season, fitness is all in the head not the body.

The body needed work too, of the soothing variety. James Robson, a Cumbrian who has spent many years working with Scotland's various teams, was to make his third successive Lions tour as doctor, a man who was on constant call. Mark Davies, a former Swansea captain, was again Lions physiotherapist, and Richard Wegrzyk, masseur. Two of Lenihan's travelling partners from days with the Ireland team, baggage manager Pat O'Keefe and administrative assistant Joan Moore, were also signed up. The final part of the jigsaw was Alex Broun as media liaison officer. He was to keep the media in line, an unenviable task with the exception of dealings with *The Daily Telegraph*.

Mark Taylor (centre) made the squad of 37 ahead of Swansea and Wales team-mate Scott Gibbs (left).

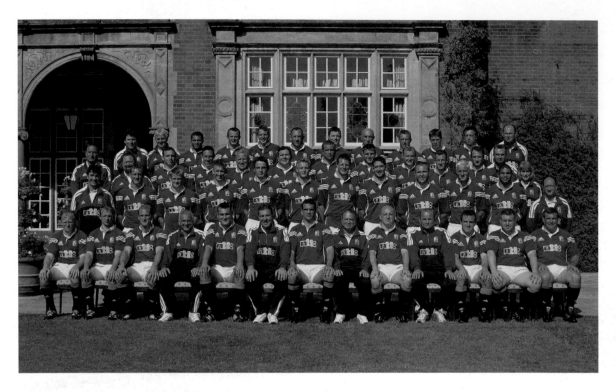

All part of the team. The British and Irish Lions party to Australia 2001, including management and support staff.

The mood that day was upbeat. As it should have been. It was an exciting adventure. Everyone knew what they were letting themselves in for. The Wallabies had got the royal flush of sporting honours: world champions, Tri-Nations champions, Bledisloe Cup holders. They were on their own turf. And they were driven by a nation that had come to expect success.

'Australia is the number one nation for sport in the world,' said Henry. 'The USA might take exception to that notion but that's the way it is to my mind in terms of their relative populations. There is a real culture for sport in the country and it comes through at all levels. They have got attitude and they have got the infrastructure to bring that attitude through. They want to be the best, no matter what the sport might be. You saw that at the Sydney Olympics. They have tremendous self-belief and a desire to express themselves through sport. It might pain me to say this as a New Zealander but in the last few years they have become the best rugby country in the world, maximising their resources. What greater challenge could there be than to be involved in that?'

What indeed? The squad had been named, the plans made, the letters sent out. Everything was in place. The itinerary had eventually been thrashed out. It had taken nine drafts to agree the schedule with the Australian Rugby Union, with both sides looking for the slightest edge. The Australians wanted to place the three Super-12 sides on successive Saturdays. The Lions wanted a loosener before they got into the heavy-duty stuff. They got their way. The ten-match tour was to start in Perth on 8 June against Western Australia.

It was now 25 April. The Lions were to assemble at Tylney Hall just outside Basingstoke in a little over four weeks' time. There were 18 players from England, ten from Wales, six from Ireland and three from Scotland. 'Never mind where they come from,' said Lenihan. 'They will be Lions the moment they step across the threshold of Tylney Hall.'

All looked set fair. Four weeks to go. 'This is the end of the beginning,' said Millar. A good line for what was shaping up to be a great trip.

The ultimate conversion.

The world's first fully flat beds in business class.
New Club World.

 member

 **BRITISH AIRWAYS**

Being introduced across the network.

THE TOSCANINI SUITE

THE WORLD'S MOST DISCREET DIGITAL CAMCORDER

JVC VIDEO LENS
F:3.7~37 F1.8 / 10x

JVC
100x
DIGITAL ZOOM

Camera shown actual size

miniature™
THE WORLD'S MOST DISCREET DIGITAL CAMCORDER

Your relationship with your camcorder may never be the same again. The new JVC miniature™ is the smallest and lightest digital camcorder in the world. Being miniature there are no limits to where you will choose to use it. Every element of digital technology you could ever wish for is fitted as standard. How discreet will you choose to be?

Digital stills camera built in • Removable SD Memory card (8MB) • Video clips for e-mail • MP3 digital sound effects • 2"colour LCD screen • Models available - GR-DVP1 silver / GR-DVP3 black (DV input)

JVC

2. Early Games

The tables were dotted around, each with a little flagpole bearing a name. There were flagpoles in the gardens, flagpoles in the oak-panelled library, flagpoles in the high-windowed drawing room. Flagpoles everywhere. Journalists too. TV cameramen strode across the manicured lawns, pausing only to grab a cup of coffee from the starched-shirted waiters standing diligently by. Phew, it's a rough old trade is following rugby!

The media open day at Tylney Hall, a beautifully restored country house hotel set in acres of finest Hampshire countryside, was like a scene from *Brideshead Revisited*. It was as far removed from the muddied depths of winter as it was possible to get. And that is precisely what the Lions had to leave behind. The personnel belonged to another time. The fierce rivalries of the Six Nations Championship, the spats, the jibes, the wind-ups

It is the end of May 2001, and press day unfolds at Tylney Hall, Hampshire, venue for the Lions team-building programme.

and even the occasional punch-ups, had no place at Tylney Hall. The players may well have spent many moments visualising how many lumps they were going to knock out of each other wearing the colours of their country. Now they had to spend many hours visualising how they were to become blood brothers in six days.

The Arcadian delights of Tylney Hall were deceptive. Sure there was a lot of fun and games to be had there. But it was serious fun and games. There was also some hard training to be done – isn't there always hard training to be done? – at the Army Rugby Stadium in nearby Aldershot. But the main purpose of the gathering at Tylney was to bring the squad together, for the members to get to know each other at the most basic level.

'Hello, I'm Matt Dawson. I'm a scrum half. I play for Northampton.' Sound daft? Yes, it does. But the simple handshake and namecheck was the first step. A lot of the players knew each other only by reputation. 'There are probably about one-third of the guys I don't know at all,' said Dawson (scrum half, Northampton, 28). 'Even people like Scott Murray who I've played against at Saracens. The Welsh lads such as Colin Charvis, Dafydd James, Robin McBryde I don't know, nor the Irish boys, Ronan O'Gara and Brian O'Driscoll. But it's not just

'Out came an assortment of instruments…' Danny Grewcock, Keith Wood and Neil Back make music at Tylney Hall.

successfully with Ian McGeechan four years earlier before that tour set off to South Africa. It was the same exercise here. The objective may have been the same, but the routines changed. There were various ploys used to break down barriers and get people unfamiliar with each other to be familiar with each other. One morning saw the Lions ensemble congregate in the Tylney Hall courtyard. Out came an assortment of instruments – drums, bells, tambourines, glockenspiel, maracas. The squad had one hour to make music. Away they went. Andy Robinson was on the big drum, Graham Henry on the tambourine, Lawrence Dallaglio on the glockenspiel, with fitness adviser

about pleasantries here. It's about genuine communication, about building a sense of each other and establishing trust. You've spent all that time in the season looking to drive each other into the ground. Now you've got to have that same bloke on your side, laying his body on the line for you.'

The six-day camp was overseen by Impact, a corporate group specialising in team-building and management bonding. The company had worked

Steve Black the self-appointed Rhythm King. 'All together now. One, Two, Three, Banana…' All good fun; another little step along the way to establishing an identity for the 2001 Lions.

They had their dragon-boat races, their assault course, their Jacob's Ladder high up in the air on which they had to help each other to the top across precarious links. They all linked arms and pledged themselves to the cause. As they would. There was not a man among the 37-strong party that would not have uttered undying allegiance to the Lions. Saying it and doing it are different matters, of course. The sense of togetherness, evident throughout that week when we dropped by at training at Aldershot or on that sun-dappled Open Day at Tylney, was all fine and dandy when the going was smooth. Many stories were written that week about the harmony of the group (excluding their musical talents). It would have been far more of a story if there hadn't been a sense of it – if there had been any friction or jealousies. These blokes were all desperate for it to work.

No, the test of the Impact initiative would come not in the Hampshire countryside but somewhere far across the water, on Australia's east coast, a long way from home. Only then would the Lions management find out if the Tylney days had been worthwhile. Only when the tour hit a bit of turbulence, with injury, a defeat perhaps or a dispute over selection, would the bonds be tested. Easy to wrap arms around each other and swear an oath under the Lions banner. Wait, though, until that bloke has nipped in ahead of you for Test selection and see what the reaction is. Would the old prejudices resurface? Would the squad go off into their little huddles? Would they seek the comfort and confidence of those they knew rather than those they had only just met? Good questions and no answers to be had at this stage.

It was ironic that all this structured integrating took place in the professional era. In the amateur days, when the contact between players was much less fluid, when there was no Heineken Cup or transborder competition, when the sense of enmity between the countries was deep, they could have done with some sort of formal bonding exercise. Instead they had to rely on informal means – drink. The pub was the venue used in those days to break down barriers. As the 2001 management knew only too well. 'We've been here three and a half days and no one's been to the pub yet,' said Donal Lenihan.

Praise or complaint? No one was quite sure, including Lenihan. The modern rugby player may well reach for the isotonic glug and protein mix long before he would lunge for a pint of the dark stuff. But they do have their moments.

'We are climbing Jacob's Ladder…' Donal Lenihan, Neil Jenkins and friends provide mutual support in the treetops.

There was simply no time at that point to do anything but work and work. The play could wait. A few of the players were still feeling their way back to fitness. Lawrence Dallaglio was written off by almost everyone except one key individual – himself. He damaged his knee playing for Wasps against Bath in the semi-finals of the Zurich play-offs. There was talk of possible cruciate damage. Dallaglio thought otherwise, and a second medical opinion gave him the benefit of any doubt. He was fit to tour, although he would not be ready for action until the second or third week. Still, he managed to take part in many of the routines. 'We're going to give him as much time as he needs,' said Lenihan. 'For a player of that quality it's the thing to do.'

The Bank Holiday Monday session at Aldershot was a hard slog. Andy Robinson did much of the barking and shouting, driving the players to work hard at their contact drills. At the other end of the

Kicking coach Dave Alred looks on as Neil Jenkins swings into action in pre-tour training at Aldershot.

field Phil Larder was getting to work – organising, directing, setting out the crucial areas of the defensive patterns that the Lions were to use. His ideas were familiar to the England and Leicester players. They were totally alien to all the rest. It might have been easier if they had all been starting from scratch. But of all the elements that had to be refined, defence was the most important. A fluffed line-out call will cost you possession – important but not necessarily fatal. A missed tackle at international level is always fatal.

'We all need to be singing from the same hymn sheet,' said Larder. 'If there is just one doing something just slightly different, then we will have massive problems. Take Jonny Wilkinson. He's one of the best tacklers I've ever come across. Yet when he first came into the England set-up he was all at sea in one game against Scotland simply because he was more in tune with the Newcastle way of doing things. It's not a question of technical ability.

It's a question of organisation. For that you need communication and trust. It's a massive challenge, as big a one as I've faced in sport.'

The week fizzed by. The players were all out to impress. Every little moment counted, every little gesture would be noted by someone – even if only at a subconscious level. 'Mind you, there are times when you have to switch off,' said Dawson. 'You'd drive yourself mad otherwise.'

One or two players were not able to play much part in training. Wales prop Dai Young had a calf strain, while Iain Balshaw was still getting over the collarbone injury he too had picked up in the play-offs. His Bath team-mate Mike Catt was also sitting out with a bad back. He said that he felt fine otherwise. The slight frown suggested another tale. Again, he was given the benefit of the doubt.

News filtered through from Australia that all the Tests, at the Gabba in Brisbane, the Colonial Stadium in Melbourne and Stadium Australia in Sydney, had sold out within minutes of going on sale. The Aussies seemed surprised by this. The Brits and Irish were not. Thousands were packing their bags to head south. By Thursday afternoon it was time for the players to begin packing their bags. They were booked on flight SQ317 out of Heathrow bound for Perth via Singapore the next day at noon. Their wives, partners and families came along to Tylney Hall to say their farewells.

'The boys were a bit flat at training today,' said Lions coach Graham Henry. 'It's an emotional time. They knew their families were coming along and it made them suddenly realise what was about to happen. They were apprehensive about getting an injury at this stage. As it is they're getting on the plane tomorrow, all 37 of them, and that's good news. It's been a good week in all aspects. I thought we'd only be at about 25 per cent. Instead we're around 50 per cent. There's a buzz about, an edge and an atmosphere. Exciting stuff, isn't it?'

Alongside Henry at the final press conference on home soil sat Martin Johnson, a man who'd been round rugby's blocks a few times. He's not a man given to much emotional statement. He'd captained a Lions squad to South Africa and taken it all in his significant stride. And yet you could sense in Johnson that he too was much taken by the prospect of flying down into the Aussies' backyard and giving them a bloody nose.

'I think you do get more excited as you get older if only because you know that this might be your last chance,' said Johnson. 'In my case it most certainly will be. It doesn't matter that I've been on a Lions trip before. This is the 2001 Lions – new faces and new ideas. The eagerness to get on with the job is as high as it could be.'

And off they went, in pursuit of their personal goals and collective dreams. They knew that it was to be a crash-bang-wallop trip, that there was little time to make their mark. If they needed a short cut to finding out about any of their band of Lions brothers they could have browsed through the very impressive media guide put together by Alex Broun. All life was in those pages, although the sharp ones had already anticipated how it would read in print.

Martin Johnson: How would you describe your character? *Very dull.*

What would you be if you weren't a professional rugby player? *An amateur rugby player.*

How do you prepare for a big match? *Get changed into my rugby kit.*

There were other nuggets:

Colin Charvis: Which other sportsperson do you most admire? *Emile Zatopek.* Good choice.

Dan Luger: What would you like to be if you weren't a professional rugby player? *A pro surfer.*

He would have a chance to test that out when the team reached Sydney. They were to stay at the Manly Pacific, literally a stone's throw from one of the city's most famous surfing beaches.

The favourite books ranged from Alan Clark's *Diaries*, nominated by Scotland prop Tom Smith; a very highbrow (and good) read, *The Human Stain*, chosen by Wales centre Mark Taylor; and *Ham on Rye* by Charles Bukowski, which was the choice of Scotland No. 8 Simon Taylor. Keith Wood's favourite music included Bob Dylan, Lou Reed and Leonard Cohen, music for every mood; that of Brian O'Driscoll was Stereophonics and Coldplay; Red Hot Chilli Peppers and Crowded House were the choice of lock Jeremy Davidson.

There was one other thing to do on the 20-hour trip to Perth – rest. There was not going to be too much of that over the next fortnight. The last Lions tour was the same. As they left, the common cry from all quarters was that after such a demanding season the one thing that the players needed was rest. They were battered physically and mentally.

Dream on. If it had been a national team then it would have been relatively easy to fit in some down time when the players could soothe their aches and pains and get their heads back together. On a Lions tour there is no time for such luxuries or even essentials. The Lions are a scratch side. They need every second available to get the whole squad on the same wavelength – on the Larder wavelength, on the scrum wavelength, on the line-out wavelength, on the ruck and maul... You get the picture. And all this while mixing and matching the combinations, seeing who can cut it and who can't, who works well with each other and who doesn't. International teams are settled; Lions teams are in a state of constant flux.

While they shuffled and jigged, the Wallabies set up camp at Coffs Harbour in northern New South Wales and got on with doing what most of them had been doing together for the last couple of years – drills, drills and drills. They would not lose through a lack of understanding – boredom, maybe; anything else, no way. Nothing was left to chance in the Wallaby mindset.

Not that it would be with the Lions. It's just that time was at a premium. And that again is why the Lions have such a special aura. The challenge is huge and the pitfalls many. But if it comes off, the feeling is one of the best there is to be had in sport.

The feeling the players had when they did get to their first base in Australia, the Esplanade Hotel in Fremantle, was none too clever. They were off the plane and out to the training pitch. Next morning, at 7.30 a.m., they were out there again. It was also raining on arrival. Welcome to Australia! It was also midnight on their body clocks. The players were not slow to point this out to the management. The management were not slow to respond. They changed the early start but still two sessions a day was the bare minimum.

'Off the plane and out to the training pitch…' Tackling practice at Fremantle ahead of the tour opener against Western Australia.

The Lions based themselves down at Fremantle to give themselves time and space. The port is about ten miles out of Perth and is a renowned boating town from where the famous Alan Bond America's Cup bid was successfully launched in the mid-1980s. The Lions were to have little joy at escaping the throng. Word soon leaked out as to where they were. They were hot news. They were also a hot target for the Wallabies. One of their legion of coaches was spotted filming one of their training sessions. The shutters came down. Training sessions became closed affairs.

The media rolled into town for the first team announcement. The first match was against Western Australia at the WACA on Friday 8 June. The team had had six days to acclimatise. Brian O'Driscoll would have 80 minutes to acclimatise to the role of full back. The naming of the first team on any tour is always a lively affair. Even if there is not much to be read into the line-up, every last nuance will always be extracted. Several rain forests had been felled for the paper on which the endless tour previews had been written. Finally this was the real thing – a proper Lions line-up, not more conjecture about what might happen.

O'Driscoll was the talking point. The Leinster centre, the rave of the Irish rugby scene, the scorer of a hat-trick of tries in Paris the previous season, the pre-tour so-called certainty for the outside centre slot, had been chosen at full back. And how many times had he ever played there? 'Never,' said O'Driscoll. What was the thinking? 'We just wanted to look at our options further down the line,' said Henry. 'If we have a Test 22 and don't have a specialist full back on the bench then we want to see who can play there. You shouldn't read any more than that into it.'

Fat chance. The conspiracy machine cranked into action. So the Lions are worried about their back three, are well stocked with centres, so move O'Driscoll back, put Mark Taylor at outside centre, move Iain Balshaw to wing… Tongues wagged and pieces were penned.

There were other points of passing interest. Rob Howley got first shout at scrum half, a position that was to be hotly contested with Matt Dawson and Austin Healey. Howley was right back to the top of

Rookie full back Brian O'Driscoll gives the Western Australia defence the slip during the Lions 116-10 victory at the WACA.

his form after the gloom of 18 months earlier when he was stripped of the captaincy and then dropped by Wales. 'The captaincy was inhibiting him a little bit,' said Henry, the man who did the stripping and dropping. 'Rob is a natural game breaker and I wanted to give him that freedom back. I think that quality is back in his game.'

Keith Wood, whose father Gordon played for the 1959 Lions, was to have the honour of leading out the 2001 Lions. Tour captain Martin Johnson was to be held back for bigger battles. Johnson had had a demanding season as Leicester went for honours on three fronts. He himself was champing at the bit, but he recognised the value in what was being proposed. 'It's a great honour, of course, something that will probably really only hit home when I'm an old fellow looking back,' said Wood. 'To be honest, the main thing is that we're all just looking forward to getting stuck into a match.'

And O'Driscoll? What did his national captain think of that one? 'I've no doubt he will go well,' said Wood. 'He has exceptional talent.'

Which is more than could be said for Western Australia. Their Thursday night training session held up at Palmyra RFC at Tompkins Park was revealing. Several shrewd observers, with spread-betting accounts back in the UK, rushed to the phone that night and enquired on the victory spread being forecast for the Lions. '60-62 points,' came the reply. The boys plunged. They knew a good-value bet when they heard one. WA were a scratch side. And a bunch of amateurs. Literally so. They were a collection of bricklayers, mechanics, roofers, engineers – all those familiar entries that used to accompany pen pictures of British and Irish players. Those were the amateur days. WA, with 11 Kiwis in their ranks, were on a hiding to nothing. 'If I were a betting man I wouldn't be betting on us,' said Duncan McRae, the former Saracens fly half, now back in Australia and one of two outsiders drafted in for the game.

How fitting then that the match should be played at the WACA, home to the Western Australian Cricket Association. The summer sport was all around. Pictures of Dennis Lillee and Rod Marsh had pride of place in the Tompkins Park pavilion, which also hosts cricket. The WACA itself reeked of great cricketing feats.

Richard Hill and hat-trick man Scott Quinnell ring down the curtain on a Western Australian attack in Perth.

The Lions managed one themselves, racking up 116 points. They didn't have the option of declaring. WA did what they could. They certainly did not want for effort, but they were hopelessly outgunned. They did have the minor consolation of scoring two second-half tries through Brent Becroft and Robbie Barugh – blemishes that were noted by the Lions defence coach – to make the final score 116-10. As for the rest of the evening there were plenty among the crowd of 20,695 streaming away

Simon Taylor runs in a try on his Lions debut v Western Australia. A knee injury suffered in the match ended the 21-year-old's tour.

from a rain-sodden WACA wondering if it had all been worthwhile. The players had hit a groove, running in 18 tries and posting a record score for any British and Irish Lions side, eclipsing the 97-point mark registered against SW Districts at Mossel Bay, South Africa, in 1974. Willie John McBride's boys had a few more games in which to limber up and could afford the occasional gentle run-out. Could the 2001 Lions? That would not be known until the final whistle of the third Test had been blown. There were hat-tricks for Dan Luger and Scott Quinnell, a couple of tries apiece for Neil Back, Iain Balshaw and Rob Howley.

It was no more than a run-out for the players and did not test their patterns in the slightest. It was better than a full contact training session but not by much. Henry made all the right diplomatic noises afterwards about how important it was to keep rugby on the map in this part of the world. He knew inside that the game had virtually been a waste of time.

Lions tours have always had a missionary element, an obligation to take the game around the country and spread the word. But as tours get shorter and shorter, there is no longer slack in the system. The scale of the defeat would have been noted in home union committee rooms for the next scheduled trip to these parts in 12 years' time. This was the fourth time the Lions had come visiting, having won 71-3 in 1930, 60-3 in 1966 and 44-0 in 1989. Would the Lions come again?

It would be a pity if not, for Perth is a fine city, standing proudly on the Swan River. The players would have had little time for exploring. The media were to do that for them, invited out for a regatta on the river on the morning of the match. There were five boats, all skippered by experienced hands, veterans of the demanding Sydney–Hobart race. Under grey skies, the media pack must have

Painting Perth red. Lions coach Graham Henry celebrates his birthday after the win over Western Australia.

been fallen on midway through the second half and taken a bit of a knock on his knee. He thought nothing of it. However, good man that he is, he thought he had better just mention to the medical staff that he'd had a bang so that he could ice it up properly. One look from Lions doctor James Robson was enough to set alarm bells ringing. By midnight that Friday Donal Lenihan was on the phone to Canada to summon Leicester forward Martin Corry from the England tour. With one No. 8, Lawrence Dallaglio, already laid up and another looking in bad order, Lenihan was taking no chances. The news did not go down well across the Pacific Ocean. England manager Clive Woodward accused the Lions of panicking. 'I thought Clive Woodward had the franchise on panicking' was the reply of Donal Lenihan the next day. Ouch!

Taylor had a grade two tear in his medial ligament. There was also damage to his anterior cruciate. An MRI scan at 7.30 on the Saturday morning confirmed the bad news.

The squad was to up sticks for the long trek across Australia that day, from the southwest fringe to the north Queensland coast at Townsville. By scheduled flight via Adelaide, Sydney and Brisbane it is a back-breaking 14-hour slog. By charter plane, an 80-seater out of Perth's domestic airport with a brief refuelling stopover at Alice Springs, it was a five-and-a-half-hour journey. So much for the theory. The plane was not fit to fly because of a navigational problem. There were also problems with the weight of the Lions luggage. There were also… problems. Funny how the list of excuses can stretch out. The upshot was that the squad was delayed on the ground for over six hours. They had been due to depart at midday. It was almost 6.30 p.m. by the time their plane took off.

Simon Taylor was not with them. He had intended to come to Townsville and head for home from there. The delays put paid to that plan. As the party headed through Departures, a very disorientated Taylor took leave of his brief acquaintances. One by one they came up to shake his hand. Taylor took it all in seeming good cheer, not quite able to take in the surreal nature of what was happening. It had not been even 24 hours earlier that he had made his Lions debut. Now he

explored at least 100 metres of river in an hour's sailing. Ellen MacArthur could sleep easy.

That was more than could be said of Scotland No. 8 Simon Taylor. The 21-year-old tour rookie had come on in the second half and made the most of his first Lions appearance, running strongly and showing that he lacked for nothing in self-confidence. He scored a try and had a direct hand in two others. He finished the match strongly. Or appeared to do so.

By the next day he was off the tour, the first player to make that sad trudge back to the UK weighed down by unfulfilled dreams. Taylor had was going home. Cruel or what? 'I'll be crying into my pillow for a few months,' said Taylor. 'I suppose Edinburgh is not the worst city in the world to drown sorrows.' He put on a brave face. Inside his heart was bleeding.

The Lions had already suffered another injury. The day before the game, Wasps hooker Phil Greening had been bowled over at a training session. He had not even been doing contact work himself as he had a sore neck. He was standing near some tackle bags with another bystander, Mike Catt, when he was sent flying accidentally by Matt Perry and Matt Dawson. The dreaded words 'medial ligament' were uttered. The feeling was, though, that Greening might be back in action within a fortnight. Again the Lions management decided to give a player the benefit of any doubt.

'It has been depressing for the group to see two players injured in such a short space of time and in such circumstances,' said Graham Henry, who had celebrated his 55th birthday on the day of the WA game. (Some moron tipped beer on him from one of the stands at the WACA as he was doing a post-match TV interview.) 'It was a downer for the tour party but both guys showed tremendous character.' Scotland hooker Gordon Bulloch already had the call and was on his way from Vail, Colorado, USA, where he had been on a training holiday.

It was time to get out of town. If only! The players slumped around the National Jet terminal, bored and frustrated. Those that had played wanted to be able to stretch properly. A couple played scrabble, others lay on the floor to rest their legs. Only the coaching staff were able to get anything positive from the cock-up. They plugged in their computers and gadgetry and got to work on analysing what had happened the night before. The players had no such distractions on offer.

After a couple of hours, Donal Lenihan announced that the delay would be much longer than they had thought. It was back on the bus and into town for lunch and R&R at Burswood Casino Complex. Finally, shortly after darkness had fallen, the plane took off. Across the other side of Australia in Sydney, the Wallabies were having a much more strenuous workout than the Lions had managed against WA, the New Zealand Maori

pushing them all the way before the world champions came home 41-29.

The squad landed at Townsville Airport at 1.15 a.m. It was 2.30 by the time they checked into the Jupiters Hotel and Casino. When they pulled their curtains back the next morning they were able to look out across the clear blue waters, past Magnetic Island towards the distant Great Barrier Reef. Looking was as close as they were to get. It was work time again.

Townsville is in the northern tropics, a steamy, sleepy place that has undergone a major facelift in the past ten years. The seafront esplanade has been done up, and the big charter catamarans do good business shipping people out to the reef. And shipping them back again these days. The story was told of the company operating up the coast from Cairns that had taken a group out to the reef, about an hour's trip, supervised their snorkelling and diving and returned to base. Returned to base, that is, without one American who had been accidentally left behind. Oops!

There was no chance of the Lions encountering a watery grave. The matches were now to come thick and fast. There was little time to prepare, let alone relax. The side to face the Queensland President's XV was named that Sunday. Nearly everyone who was available who had not played against Western Australia was to get a run-out. Will Greenwood was paired with Rob Henderson in the centre, with Dafydd James and Jason Robinson on the wings. Matt Dawson and Neil Jenkins were selected at half back.

Martin Corry breezed into the hotel at 2.30 that afternoon, looking slightly bewildered but hugely chuffed. He'd been eating breakfast in Vancouver on Friday morning when the call came and now here he was across the ocean in northern Queensland. He had little time to reflect on it all – he was in the side to face the President's XV. 'I feel in good shape,' said Corry after his 24-hour trek with 16 hours' worth of time difference. 'I feel gutted for Simon Taylor. I can't imagine how he must be feeling.'

One man's calamity is another's opportunity. Corry was itching to show the selectors that they had been wrong to leave him out of the original squad. Martin Johnson and Jonny Wilkinson were again rested.

Several of the players watched the State of Origin rugby league game between Queensland and New South Wales on television, the second leg of the annual three-match series. NSW had been on the ropes after the first game but came back strongly to level the series. In town every bar was packed as people crowded round the TV sets. There was much singing, shouting and jumping up and down. And that was just the women.

The Lions knew that they were due a far sterner test from the Queensland President's XV, which had ten players with Super-12 experience. Dumped Wallaby prop Fletcher Dyson was out to prove a

point. 'For many of these guys it is the biggest game of their lives,' said the President's XV coach, Peter Grigg. 'A lot of them are chasing Super-12 contracts for next season so will be looking to impress. We will have the passion to test the Lions.'

Townsville was keen to put on a good show. The town was pushing to stage Super-12 fixtures at the Dairy Farmers Stadium, a 30,000-capacity ground on the outskirts and venue for the North Queensland Cowboys rugby league side. 'Show No Fear' was the rallying cry on the back page of the *Townsville Bulletin* on the morning of the game.

Well, they didn't. They were competitive and troublesome, pushing the Lions in every phase of play. Pity about the second half, though. It was a strange game, a game of two radically different halves. The Lions led only 10-6 at the break and had been forced to work hard to keep their try line

Man of the match Colin Charvis sets off on a charge against the Queensland President's XV in the Lions 83-6 win at Townsville.

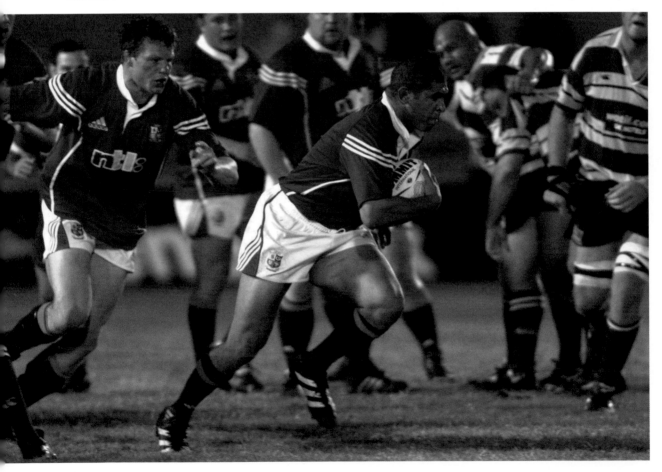

Three-try Rob Henderson gathers his own kick ahead to touch down against the Queensland President's XV.

intact. Dai Young and Colin Charvis had worked their way over for tries, with Queensland fly half Shane Drahm knocking over a couple of penalties for the home side.

The crowd of 18,653 were seeing a good contest. And then it all went horribly wrong. Charvis scored his second try of the night within 35 seconds of the restart. The floodgates were being prised open. By the time the final whistle was blown the Lions had racked up 73 second-half points without reply, a record for the Lions. Jason Robinson nabbed five scores, a decent return for a Lions debut.

'At half-time it didn't look too rosy there, did it?' said Henry afterwards. 'It was a more satisfying performance all round for us than in Perth. It was good to see people put their hands up for Test spots. We played too much as individuals in the first half but put that right after the break. Guys are a bit too anxious to make a mark but they eventually settled.'

Charvis led the way with a terrific all-round show in the back row. Greenwood and Henderson combined well in the centre, working the field and creating the space from which Robinson was to make such handsome profit. Austin Healey, when he came on at fly half for Neil Jenkins just after the hour mark, looked in good nick.

Former rugby league wing Robinson stole all the headlines, yet the guy on the other wing, Dafydd James, had also shown considerable skill at

Jason Robinson autographs shirts for fans after his five-try Lions debut at Townsville.

opening up the field. James is a classy footballer. but was just not able to finish off many of the chances created as he lacked that little bit of pace.

Robinson was the first to admit that the credit should go elsewhere. 'It's not all about me at all,' he said. 'The boys do all the hard work and it's just up to me to be patient and do the business if I get the chance. I'm still learning this game. People think I'm pulling the wool over their eyes when I say that but I'm not. I still have to pinch myself that all this is happening.'

It was. The Lions were roared on by the thousand or so fans that had already made their way out for the tour. Ireland centre Rob Henderson crowned an impressive evening's work with a hat-trick of tries; lock Malcolm O'Kelly scored as well.

A penalty try was also awarded when a line-out maul was brought down.

Eleven tries were scored in the second half as the Lions ran out 83-6 winners. 'British Blitz' said the local paper the next morning. The Wallabies were watching from their training camp in Coffs Harbour. They would have been impressed. There was a sense of steel as well as enthusiasm about the Lions play in the second half. 'It was an important moment there at half-time,' said Lenihan. 'No one panicked and that's a good sign.'

It was. It meant that some trust and understanding was building. The Lions would need all of that in the upcoming ten days. They flew to Brisbane the next afternoon. Three big predators lay in wait, looking to knock them off – Queensland Reds, Australia A and New South Wales Waratahs. Games to be won, reputations to be made or lost. The tour was hotting up.

THE LIONS.
FOUR NATIONS.
ONE SHIRT.

adidas®
FOREVER SPORT

2001.
THE IDEAL
MOTIVATION
FOR 2005.

The British and Irish Lions have never lacked the determination, hunger, ambition, passion and desire to win. And losing has only made them stronger. Roll on 2005.

3. Heavy Duty

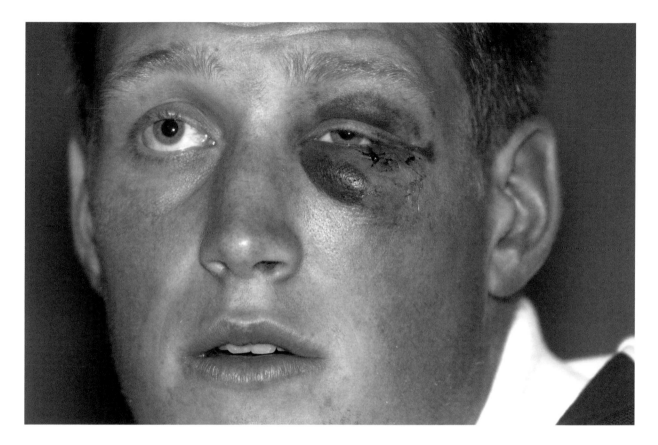

There is no steady progression on a Lions tour of Australia, just a switchback of peaks and troughs. The opposition ranges from the inept to the formidable. Only one thing is constant – the sniping. The Lions continued to be fired on from the sidelines – cheating in the line out, illegal at the scrum and villains at the breakdown.

The games on the field so far had been little more than gentle looseners. Now for the real thing. As the standard of opposition was cranked up, so was the volume of vitriol. It passed for supposedly serious debate. There was little doubt, though, that much of it was orchestrated from within. The Australians have minimal resources at their disposal. What they have, in terms of personnel and media savvy, they use to the limit.

The Lions flew down from Townsville on Wednesday afternoon, leaving behind the steamy temperatures of the northern coastline. The slight change in weather conditions did not fool them for a second. They knew that the opposition would be whipping up a storm over the next 12 days. The Lions had entered phase two of the trip. They'd had their down time, their opportunity to bond and gel. Now was the time to put all that into practice.

This was ambush time, the moment when the tourists could find themselves bushwhacked by opponents desperate to create a bit of mayhem ahead of the Test series. The Lions were to play Queensland Reds, Australia A and New South

Neil Back and Donal Lenihan make use of one of the fleet of Land Rovers made available throughout the tour.

Wales Waratahs within eight days – a tough assignment by any stretch of the imagination.

How should the management approach the games? Traditionally the Saturday fixtures on tours are the most difficult games. The Reds, Super-12 semi-finalists, were to be a good test, so too the Waratahs, even though they had only a skimpy input to the current Wallaby side. But lurking in the middle of the pack was the tricky little number up at Gosford, a 90-minute drive north of Sydney, against Australia A. That team was to be coached by Eddie Jones, Wallaby coach elect, who had been preening and steeling his men in camp for ten days. (Where would Australian rugby be without its training camps? The players spend more time there than they do out on the field of play. Still, it appears to work for them.)

The Lions named their side for the Queensland game before heading south. They opted to go for Test match practice. They denied that they had picked a shadow Test team a fortnight ahead of the first Test, but it certainly had the air of one. Tom Smith, Keith Wood and Phil Vickery hooked up in the front row, backed by Martin Johnson and Danny Grewcock. With Lawrence Dallaglio still not quite ready the favoured back row was Richard Hill and Neil Back on the flanks with Scott Quinnell at No. 8. The Welshman was forced to drop out the day before the game with fluid on the knee, to be replaced by Martin Corry. Rob Howley and Jonny Wilkinson were paired at half back, with an all-Ireland duo of Rob Henderson and Brian O'Driscoll in the centre. Dan Luger and Dafydd James were on the wings, with Iain Balshaw at full back.

Pick some holes in that little one. It was hard to do so. Jason Robinson was improving all the time, but his rightful place at this stage was on the bench. Austin Healey was there too, for the third game in succession. He wasn't too chuffed about that, but good fellow that he is, and mindful of all the oaths of allegiance to the greater good pledged at Tylney Hall, he wobbled his way along the party line.

'I suppose they're going with horses for courses,' said Healey, who'd had two stints in different positions, at scrum half and at fly half. Jack of all trades and... No, that would be grossly unfair. Healey had been sharp and inventive when slotting in at stand-off, a position he'd taken up in extremis with Leicester; he had grown into it, so much so that his devilish darts from there helped his team win the Heineken Cup. Even a man of his considerable self-belief and front would not dare to presume that he could knock Jonny Wilkinson out of the rankings. But he wanted to start, wanted to show what he could do from first whistle. It's the natural instinct of any sportsman. Coaches may bleat about their sports being a squad operation these days, that every one on the roster has an equal contribution to make. No one buys into that claptrap. Any player worth his salt wants to start. He wants to be thought the best. Healey was no different. 'I've become a bit of a joker in their thinking,' said Healey of the management. 'Someone who can come on and do something. I wouldn't mind the opportunity to start, that's all.'

Fair comment. Queensland was going to be a decent workout. The players knew that. And they knew too that if they made their mark against quality opposition then it would count for far more in the minds of the selectors than a bit of freewheeling against Western Australia.

Queensland had hoped to be at full strength. But as they prepared to name their side the signs were that they would be without captain John Eales. The Wallaby lock and skipper had aggravated his Achilles tendon while in training camp with Australia. Queensland coach Mark McBain was none too happy. 'He played four games in a row for us in the Super-12 and now he can't come up to scratch,' said McBain, a former Wallaby hooker.

If Eales's omission was forced on McBain, then his decision to drop full back Nathan Williams and reserve fly half Shane Drahm was entirely at his own prompting. McBain had been in Townsville on Tuesday night to run the rule over several of the President's XV. He had an early flight the next morning to Brisbane. Not early enough for Williams and Drahm. They were just coming through the doors of their Townsville hotel at 5 a.m. as McBain was headed in the opposite direction. Oops!

McBain had been part of the Queensland side that just lost out, 19-15, to the Lions in 1989. Queensland had toppled the Lions once before, beating Carwyn James's New Zealand-bound side in 1971. The lion mascot from that trip was on parade at Ballymore. They fancied another trophy for the top shelf.

The atmosphere had changed within a few days. There was more focus and more buzz around Ballymore than had been evident before. Time, too, for a little dig. 'McBain labels Lions boring', read the headline in *The Australian*.

The Lions had racked up 31 tries in their two matches. They had shredded opposition defences, modest as they might have been. And here was McBain dubbing them tedious. And for why? 'The rolling maul,' said McBain. 'I mean it's just not a spectacle, is it?'

The Lions, eager to work their combinations, had driven over a couple of mauls from line outs. Funny that. I thought mauls and line outs were part of rugby union. McBain backtracked on the eve of the game, claiming that he had been misquoted. Too late for the retraction. The dart had been fired.

The Lions would not have noticed the pinprick.

They were too busy sifting through the constant flow of medical bulletins. On the Friday before the Queensland game they announced that hooker Phil Greening was off the tour. Yes, his knee was responding. No, it wouldn't be right in time.

It was a curious end to the Greening saga. Here was a man who had come on tour yet not actually got to wear the shirt. So close. He might never get the chance again. The Lions management had

Queensland Reds coach Mark McBain with state skipper John Eales. McBain was reportedly critical of the Lions playing style.

Phil Greening has ice applied to his injured knee. Sadly for him he was destined not to wear the red jersey on the 2001 tour.

gathering in number and filled several sections of the famous ground. They had plenty to cheer that evening. Or certainly in the first half at least. The Lions were in tip-top form. Martin Johnson led them out for his first game; Jonny Wilkinson was seeing his first action as well.

It was a keen, physical opening, one that the Lions got stuck into. Phil Vickery was warned in the early stages by referee Stuart Dickinson. There were several little spats as each side tested out the resolve of the other. The Lions, particularly with Johnson back in harness, were not going to take a backward step.

There was far more than mere muscle to their game. They had scored five tries by the time Dickinson blew for half-time. Dan Luger, looking sharp and elusive, latched on to a splendid cross-field kick by Wilkinson to score in the 17th minute. Rob Henderson was next on the trysheet,

'Sharp and elusive' Lions wing Dan Luger on his way to score against the Queensland Reds at Ballymore.

initially bent over backwards to give Greening time to recover from the knee injury. Henry had made much play of him being the life and soul of the party. The daily briefings had invariably contained the line that he was making good progress.

Not good enough. Greening himself was confused by the sudden change of direction. 'I think it's to do with insurance or something, er, I'm not sure, feeling fine,' ran the jumble of words and emotions when he tried to give his side of the story. 'It's weird. I'm gutted.' Greening was never far away on the rest of the tour. He followed the squad down to Sydney where he was due to get some rehabilitation. In the end he hooked up with one of the tour companies as a group leader. It looked good fun. But it was no consolation whatsoever.

Greening wanted to be out where the real action was, trotting down the tunnel at Ballymore on a Saturday evening with 18,337 roaring their support one way or the other. The Barmyites were

On-song Rob Henderson is tackled by Queensland Reds Wallaby internationals Elton Flatley (No. 10) and Toutai Kefu.

capitalising on a defensive cock-up by Queensland wing Junior Pelesasa. The Wasps and Ireland centre, who had pledged himself to Munster for the following season, was in good nick.

He had been the playboy of Wasps rugby for a few seasons, always ready with a quip, always eager to party. It had done him little good in rugby terms, even if his social diary was always full. He had talent but no consistency. Ireland left him out of their World Cup squad. Time to shape up or ship out. Henderson shaped up. He hired his own personal trainer (found in the London Yellow Pages) and got himself in the groove. He had a

good game against Queensland and not just by playing the biff-bash type of rugby, crashing through the centre, that we had seen from him down the years. His kicking game was sharp, his breaks and linking work, top drawer. 'Hendo went away and reinvented himself,' said Donal Lenihan.

So he did. Dafydd James and Richard Hill were the other try scorers before the break. Within four minutes of the restart, Brian O'Driscoll had scored, the Irishman tracking a little jinking movement by

Martin Johnson keeps Reds Nic Stiles and Glenn Panoho at arm's length as argy-bargy breaks out at Ballymore.

Wilkinson and being perfectly placed to take the pass and score. Significantly O'Driscoll had managed to shake off his marker, Daniel Herbert, the supposed rock of the Wallaby midfield. Every little helps in the psychological stakes.

The score stood at 39-3 at that point. It was all over. The Lions lost their shape somewhat after that. Rob Howley had taken several heavy knocks from Toutai Kefu and was forced off with a popped rib cartilage eight minutes into the second half. A Wilkinson penalty was the only score after that point. 'We were a bit fortunate with the scoreline,' said Graham Henry afterwards. 'We won't get carried away with that.' Martin Johnson was of similar mind. 'We were satisfied in some areas,' he said. 'But we turned over too much ball.'

The key thing was that the Lions had finally got the workout they needed. 'We needed a hard, physical game and we got one,' said Henry. For all Henry's reservations there was no concealing his pleasure about several of the performances.

'Jonny Wilkinson navigated the ship well and kept their defence honest,' said Henry. 'That was a big game out there for a guy who hasn't played for six weeks. And as for Martin Corry, what a fabulous game he had. I think he was telling the Lions selectors that they made a mistake by leaving him out of the original squad.'

The party checked out of the Sheraton next day, bound for Sydney and in good heart. They'd faced their first major challenge and come through. Any squad needs a proper shakedown on the field if it is to really come together. All the little gimmicks in the world count for nought if you can't trust the guy alongside you to stand firm when the fur and the fists are flying. The Lions stood firm. 'We were there toe to toe,' said Howley. 'They started it and we stood up to it.'

Could they do the same against Australia A? This was a fiendishly difficult fixture. The Lions had stacked the side against Queensland with seasoned performers. The midweek side was far less experienced and settled. There were also a couple of individuals whose minds were on personal

Richard Hill, supported by Keith Wood, takes on Reds hooker Michael Foley during the Lions 42-8 victory in Brisbane.

milestones. Mike Catt, who had been struggling since the squad assembled to shake off first a back strain and then a calf injury, was to play in the centre with Will Greenwood. In the pack, Lawrence Dallaglio was to see his first action since hurting his knee in the championship play-off match between Wasps and Bath. Scott Quinnell had recovered from the fluid on the knee. Healey finally got his wish with a start at scrum half, paired with Neil Jenkins.

The team had a vigorous run-out on Monday morning at the Manly Oval, a famous little ground just a decent punt behind the team's seafront hotel,

where the Pacific rollers crashed to shore day and night. Mike Catt seemed to be favouring his injured leg but got through training – just. He came to the sidelines and applied a mound of ice to the calf.

It was a good workout, with Phil Larder and Andy Robinson putting the non-playing group through their paces on the scrum machine and in tackling drills. The winter sun shone, and the grunts of endeavour told their own tale. The clutch of onlookers included Munster coach Declan Kidney, who was over for a couple of weeks monitoring players and trading coaching tips.

He would have learnt a thing or two about having to cope with the daily wind-ups on various fronts. Australia A coach Eddie Jones was ever present in the sports pages in the build-up, stirring and probing. Jones had a view on the Queensland match. 'I was disappointed by the amount of foul play,' said Jones. 'There were a number of incidents off the ball that were disappointing. I hope the officials on Tuesday will keep a strict eye on it and take the appropriate action.'

Just in case they hadn't heard him, Jones let off another volley the morning of the game. 'Officials have to be hard on teams that resort to foul play,' said Jones in all his pomp. 'I don't think the officials last Saturday night did that. Don't tell me that some of the blokes that resorted to foul play should not have been put in the sin bin and I mean players from both teams. There has been a constant pattern in how the Lions have played on tour and they are going to try to assert their physical superiority. They do have a master plan in place.'

If so, it wasn't clear to the Lions just who it was they were supposed to be ganging up on. They played hard, they stood their ground but there was not a shred of evidence that any of it had been premeditated. 'If you watch the video carefully it is beyond me how we can be accused of causing problems,' said Donal Lenihan. 'You can make your own mind up why they are coming out with statements like this.'

A New Zealand referee, Paul Honiss, was to take charge of the Australia A game. The Lions left their Manly hotel around midday. Gosford lies about 90 kilometres north of Sydney along the Pacific Highway. The team bus weaved its way through Sydney's sprawling northern suburbs. A

A thoughtful Lawrence Dallaglio sits out his time after being yellow-carded for persistent infringement against Australia A.

Australia A's Justin Harrison beats Scott Murray to the ball at Gosford. The Lions struggled in the line out and at the restart.

The NorthPower Stadium, a modern, appealing 20,000-capacity ground, is home to the Northern Eagles rugby league side. You drop down into the town from the Highway, snaking down through the surrounding woodland, across Brian McGowan Bridge and into the complex. Another good crowd of just under 20,000 had gathered, many of them having a bite to eat beforehand in the impressive Central Coast League Club, essentially the town's social club where all manner of supporters come for a good-value meal and a pre-match chat. It was a splendid example of a community tied in closely to its sport.

The locals got value for money that night. They cheered their boys to a very significant and thoroughly deserved 28-25 victory. The Lions were not at the races. All the power and controlled aggression of Saturday night had disappeared. The pack, with Malcolm O'Kelly and Scott Murray at lock, struggled to lay hands on the ball at restarts. Referee Honiss whistled them to distraction too at the breakdown, so denying the Lions any chance of building momentum. The final penalty count was 24-11 against the Lions, 14-4 in the first half. The Lions were sloppy all over the field, lacking in drive and co-ordination. Dallaglio, despatched to the sin bin late in the game for persistent infringement, was feeling his way back into action, while it was obvious from the early stages that Catt was not going to go the distance.

The inevitable happened just before half-time, when Catt pulled up short following up a kick through. He trudged off knowing that his tour was over. There were problems all over the field. Neither hooker, Robin McBryde nor Gordon Bulloch, could find their line-out jumpers with any consistency. It was a poor night, for several personnel as well as for tour morale. From the moment that Honiss sounded the blast that brought the match to a close, the 2001 Lions would be unable to say that they were unbeaten. No longer could they aspire to emulate Willie John McBride's 1974 tourists to South Africa. Perhaps the landmark is beyond the scope of nearly every touring side.

The end of the line for Mike Catt, as he is led off by Lions tour doctor James Robson after breaking down against Australia A.

snapshot of Sydney reveals the harbour's blue waters with its famous landmarks. All very serene, all very uncongested. The reality is the reality of all big, 21st-century cities, a metropolis choked by traffic battling through its outskirts. The Lions bus went bumper to bumper with the rest of them until it finally hit the Highway.

Australia A fly half and goal kicker Manny Edmonds is tackled by Austin Healey. Edmonds contributed 23 points to his side's win.

Nonetheless it has to be a target for every one of them as they leave home.

The midweek side is by definition and circumstance confined to the margins of the tour. The players within it have to be strong characters, stronger in many ways than those that make the Test team, for it is easy to remain online and motivated when the attention is focused on you.

There was a sense that night that the tour was slipping away from a few people. The two hookers had a hard time of it, so too the locks. Neil Jenkins did not look comfortable at all, no surprise perhaps when his knees had been troubling him all tour.

Australia A, with several Wallabies in their ranks, were well drilled and hungry. If only they had had some decent finishers in the back line, they would have been away over the horizon by half-time. As it was they lost the one dangerous runner they had, full back Richard Graham, after a clattering collision with Ben Cohen in the 25th minute. Graham was stretchered off with concussion. Inside centre Nathan Grey, pushing for a Wallaby Test spot, was forceful up through the middle. The Lions just about kept them at bay, Australia A relying on the boot of fly half Manny Edmonds to get a return for all their territorial advantage. The Waratahs fly half landed five penalty goals to two from Jenkins to send Australia A into the break 15-6 ahead. It was well deserved.

The second-row pairing of Justin Harrison and Tom Bowman ruled the roost, setting the platform for No. 8 Jim Williams and blind-side flanker David Lyons to crash forward.

There were some straws that the Lions could clutch at. For all the pressure, they did concede only one try, to Scott Staniforth in the 58th minute, the Waratah back touching down after Graeme Bond had cut inside Ben Cohen to split the defence. The Lions did also manage to stage a late rally, scoring three tries in the final quarter through Mark Taylor, Matt Perry and Jason Robinson, the last two coming in injury time. Matt Dawson had come on and taken over the kicking duties when Jenkins was substituted on the hour. He missed one straight pot at goal in the 79th minute. Those three points might (only might, for games take on a different shape depending on scores) have helped the Lions draw the match. It would not have been deserved.

The Lions management made no attempt to disguise their disappointment. 'Our line out was unacceptable and we lacked basic sharpness,' said Graham Henry. 'This is a reality check for us to show us where our baseline has to be set. This will tell us what the tour is all about. If we can learn resolve from it, then maybe it will benefit us in the long term. The dressing shed was a morgue. This could be a defining moment. Better to strike reality now than in the first Test.'

Henry did point out that it is very hard to get a Tuesday side in shape when Sunday is often a travel day. It was a stark admission. He carried on when pressed to explain that he didn't think that it was possible to give due attention to the needs of the midweek team. And what was the implication

Centre Mark Taylor, on as replacement for the injured Mike Catt, touches down during the Lions fightback against Australia A.

Darren Morris surfing at Manly beach, Sydney. The prop got the nod on the loose-head for the match against NSW Waratahs.

of that? 'That perhaps we might have to concentrate more on the Tests than on the other guys,' said Henry, making a statement that was completely at odds with the musketeer ethos of 'one for all, all for one' that had been the Lions theme ever since they had gathered at Tylney Hall. 'We need quality time and we just don't have it.'

But no Lions tour has. That is the unique challenge of them. International teams have it easy by comparison, already in tune with each other when they arrive. Those teams simply need a bit of tweaking. The Lions are something else entirely.

Was Henry about to abandon the midweek men to their fate? They still had two matches to go, against New South Wales Country Cockatoos and a depleted ACT Brumbies. It appeared that way. Henry reiterated his thoughts the following day. 'We'll make the Test team a priority,' he said. 'There's where we have to put the time in. The Tuesday side is disadvantaged. That's a reality. We need to put our eggs in the Test basket.'

Whatever the reality of the situation behind closed doors on the training field, it would still have been better to maintain a public front of collective togetherness. As it was, Henry was running the risk of driving a wedge between the midweek players and the rest. The 1997 Lions had set great store by their unity. It was a very significant moment for the whole group when the 'dirt trackers' went up to Bloemfontein and whipped the Free State. It gave the Test team, who had stayed behind in Durban to prepare for the second Test, a great boost. You had to have sympathy for the difficulties that Henry faced. Even so, it was not politic to articulate them.

A tour moves on so quickly at this stage. There is no time to mope or dwell, only to react. The Aussie media did not make too much of the setback. They recognised that very few of the players from that night would be featuring in the Test team. Sure enough, come Wednesday evening, the side to face NSW Waratahs that Saturday at the Sydney Football Stadium showed wholesale changes. Dallaglio was to get another chance to build his fitness. Darren Morris had jumped into pole position at loose-head, while it looked as if Will Greenwood was very much in the box seat at inside centre, particularly when it was confirmed that Mike Catt was off the tour.

Injuries are an inevitable part of touring. Even so, they can have a draining effect on any party. Catt, who had had such an outstanding Six Nations, had not looked right from the outset. 'I don't think I could have lived with myself if I hadn't given it a go,' said Catt, disappointed yet also relieved. 'It's a wrench to go off tour but in a way I'm glad it's now all out in the open and over. It's been a bad couple of weeks. It's been mentally very, very hard, to be part of the tour but not be part of the tour. My back was always the problem. I almost didn't make it at all, but the medics at Bath thought that the spasms would work themselves out. It got to the stage when it was almost embarrassing to be on the tour. I'm just relieved now that it's sorted, that Scott Gibbs is on his way out. He'll do a better job than I was able to do in the state that I was in.'

Within 24 hours the Lions were sending for another replacement. Dan Luger had clashed heads with Neil Back at training and fractured his cheekbone. The news was confirmed on Friday. Luger was out, Ireland's Tyrone Howe was on his way and Jason Robinson was brought off the bench to face the Waratahs. The woes were mounting. 'It's a big blow to lose two such guys within two days of each other,' said Lenihan. 'Dan was having a magnificent tour.'

Luger was devastated. He had only just made the trip after spending three months working his way back to fitness following damage to a nerve in his neck during England's match against Wales in February. He'd had the same the year before, when he was injured during the 1999 World Cup and had to battle through the rest of the season to make, at the last gasp, England's tour to South Africa.

No hard feelings. A training-ground shunt with Neil Back left Dan Luger with a fractured cheekbone, nipping his tour in the bud.

Referee Scott Young condemns Waratahs full back Duncan McRae to an early shower for his assault on Ronan O'Gara.

Luger had laughed off suggestions only seven days earlier that he was somehow jinxed. 'No. It might seem that way because I get crocked in high-profile situations,' said Luger, a popular figure whose finishing prowess (13 tries in 20 international games) would be sorely missed by the Lions.

The build-up to the Waratahs game followed its usual path. The local papers gave space to yet another dig at the Lions. This time it was Wallaby coach Rod Macqueen who weighed in with his ten cents' worth, claiming that the Lions had fully deserved to be so heavily penalised by Paul Honiss. 'I have no sympathy for them,' said Macqueen. 'They deserved it. The laws say that you cannot twist the scrum until the ball comes and they have been doing that. Also the jumper is being impeded in the line out while he's got the ball and before he is returned to the ground. There is a law that says you can't be touched until you've come down. It's a safety issue.'

It was a pathetic issue. Macqueen was essentially advocating a non-contact line out, a free lift and jump and service to the scrum half. It was a feeble effort. Even if he'd been able to hoodwink local referees, there was little chance of him being able to influence experienced Test match officials. The Wallabies were already running fearful of the fact that the likes of Martin Johnson and Danny Grewcock might be able to get into their line out and disrupt it.

Former Wallaby coach, the Waratahs' Bob Dwyer, a man more than familiar with northern hemisphere ways from his time at Leicester and Bristol, was bent on some pre-match baiting. 'The Lions do a lot of illegal things at the breakdown,' said Dwyer. 'If the Lions don't want to give away penalties then they should stop doing illegal things. Their whole defensive pattern is based on slowing down the play at the breakdown. I was really surprised that there weren't more yellow cards at Gosford.'

If Dwyer liked the sight of yellow, then he didn't have to wait long at the Sydney Football Stadium for his first fix. NSW second row Tom Bowman was sin-binned after just four seconds for raising his elbow into Danny Grewcock's face when chasing the ball at the kick-off. Referee Scott Young had no hesitation in pulling out the card and sending a shocked Bowman to the sidelines.

It was a dramatic start to what was to prove to be an explosive evening. And what a backdrop there was for it! The Sydney Football Stadium was packed to the rafters, the first time that the ground had been full to its 42,000 capacity for a non-Test match since it first opened its gates in the 1980s. It sits adjacent to the Sydney Cricket Ground and is a consumer-friendly site with all the watering holes that nearby bohemian Paddington has to offer.

There was plenty of watering done that night as fans chewed the fat over events. Five players were sin-binned in all, and one sent off. Waratahs full back Duncan McRae was shown the red card by Young in the 56th minute for a vicious, cowardly

Phil Vickery and Danny Grewcock do their stint in the sin bin at the same time as the Waratahs Brendan Cannon and Cameron Blades.

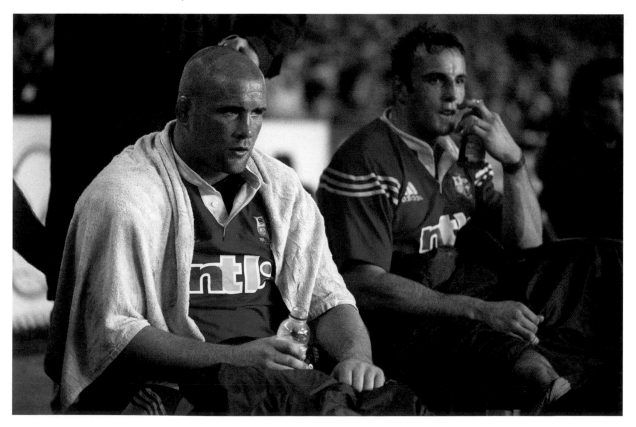

Back-rowers Neil Back and Stu Pinkerton vie for loose ball during the Lions' 41-24 victory over the Waratahs.

assault on Lions replacement Ronan O'Gara. The Irishman had come on midway through the first half for Will Greenwood and had just hit the side of a ruck near the Waratahs line when McRae struck.

McRae, who had spent much of the season wearing the colours of Saracens in London, pinned O'Gara to the floor and landed 11 punches on the defenceless player. He was eventually dragged clear. When O'Gara was pulled up, the damage was there for all to see – a gaping, streaming double laceration under the left eye. McRae even had the brass neck to smile in disbelief as Young pulled the red card from his pocket. Next day, McRae was suspended for seven weeks. He was lucky it wasn't seven weeks in prison.

The game had been on a knife edge throughout. Once again the Lions had to withstand a fearful battering from an opposition hell bent on

making a few pointed statements seven days ahead of the Test. Some of this was legitimate; some was not. The Lions were no angels themselves but nor were they a side that set out to rough up the opposition. In the era of sin bins and citing commissioners the players have too much to lose.

The niggle went on and on. It was bound to spill over into something more ugly and sustained. Sure enough it did. First McRae got his marching orders, then it was the turn of four players (two from each side) to head to the sin bin. Just three minutes after the O'Gara incident, Grewcock and Phil Vickery tangled with the Waratahs front-row duo of Brendan Cannon and Cameron Blades. Touch judge Stuart Dickinson intervened. He gave his advice to referee Scott Young – all four to the sin bin. 'Are you serious?' asked a somewhat incredulous Young.

He was serious. Young handled the situation and the match well. He made a few hare-brained calls and lost the plot momentarily when the sides were reduced to 13 against 12. He called for depowered scrums, then changed his mind. Lions hooker Keith Wood then had to point out to him that the Waratahs had too many players on the field. By and large, though, Young managed what was a tricky game.

The Lions had a mixed evening. They scored an important 41-24 victory but once again tailed off a bit in the second half. The Waratahs scored four tries in all, too many by far for the liking of Lions defence coach Phil Larder. However, the Lions were once again disrupted by injury. Will Greenwood damaged his ankle ligaments in the 25th minute, and O'Gara came on to fly half, with Wilkinson moving to inside centre. Even though Wilkinson had done a great job there for England when he first burst on the international scene, he had done all his recent defensive work at stand-off. The Lions did not have that same sense of unyielding resistance about them.

Mind you, they were sharp in other parts of the field. Jason Robinson confirmed that he really was a quality item in scoring two first-half tries, both of which necessitated him reading the play and making a bold decision. After that, his twinkling feet did the rest. Brian O'Driscoll opened the Lions account in the fourth minute, Robinson again proving a crucial link man.

The Lions led 24-5 at the interval and looked in reasonable order. Johnson and Grewcock had got the bit between their teeth up front and were giving some good ball to Matt Dawson, the Northampton scrum half getting a Saturday start as Rob Howley continued to nurse his ribs. But then it all faded away. The Waratahs hit the Lions hard at the start of the second half, scoring tries through Cullimore

and Harris. Then came the eruption. It seemed to knock the Waratahs out of their stride more than the Lions, who regrouped and actually came back well in the final ten minutes to score tries through Wilkinson and Dafydd James.

Inevitably, and rightly, the post-match focus was on the violence. 'This was a black night for

Right wing Dafydd James uses his strength to cross for the fifth Lions try of the night and his second of the tour so far.

Jonny Wilkinson, who spent part of the Waratahs match at inside centre, makes a break with Brian O'Driscoll at his shoulder.

rugby,' said Henry. 'There appeared to be more to it all than just a one-off outbreak. It was not good for the game at all.' Donal Lenihan was visibly angered by what had gone on. 'What happened to Ronan O'Gara was a disgrace,' he said.

Lenihan was not to be best pleased either when he heard about the Waratahs reaction to the incident and their subsequent defence of McRae at the judicial hearing on Sunday morning. The Waratahs, through Dwyer and manager Dave Gibson, claimed that their man had been provoked. 'What really annoyed me about it all was that there was no attempt to apologise,' said Lenihan. 'They were defending the indefensible. They said that McRae had been punched on the jaw in the clear-out tackle and then kicked on the ground. I have

to say that there was absolutely no video evidence to support such a claim and that the tribunal exonerated the Lions from any wrong-doing whatsoever. The Waratahs would have been better just closing the door on it all and taking their punishment.'

It had been a strenuous eight days. The Lions had lost two front-line players as well as suffering a reversal against Australia A. The backbiting and relentless sniping in the media was also proving to be a distraction at best and a real strain at worst. 'I've been astounded by what has happened over the last few weeks,' said Henry. 'It's time to put all that stuff in the background and concentrate on getting a side ready for a Test match.'

Fine sentiments. If only it were so easy. The gods above had a few more nasty twists in store for the Lions as they headed back up the coast to prepare for the first Test.

The scrum machine... from Barbados

TESCO

Supporting Schools Rugby

Tesco is delighted to be the official sponsor of the Under 16 and Under 18 English national teams for the 2001/02 season.

By supporting rugby union at grass-roots level, Tesco is helping to boost the development of our young players and helping to ensure the future success of the England senior teams.

www.tesco.com

Great games, books, music and videos – just a click away!
You can now order your favourite games, books, CDs, minidiscs, DVDs and videos from home.* Check out every CD and minidisc on UK release; great box office hits; and the nations top books! All from our fantastic warehouses! Simply place your order through our website, and we'll do the hard work for you. Each delivery costs justs £5, no matter how much you order.

*Now covering 90% of the population – check our website to see if you're covered.

Every little helps.

4. The First Test

Perspective is of little use in sport. What the hell is the point of sport if you can't get all emotional and worked up about it? It is fuelled by passion and argument and distortion. Sure, it is a triviality, but it is a significant triviality. That is one of its chief purposes – as a distraction from the real world.

The real world came crashing in on the Lions in the build-up to the first Test. It was time for things to be put firmly in perspective. The hammer blow for the Lions was not that there was more bad news on the injury front – Lawrence Dallaglio ruled out of the tour, Will Greenwood sidelined for at least the first Test – but the tragic death of their Australian liaison officer, Anton Toia. He died from a suspected heart attack while swimming on Monday afternoon. Anton, 54, was a hugely popular member of the party, a warm, comforting

and obliging figure to all comers. He had been part of a group that had gone out on a couple of whale-watching boats from Coffs Harbour on Monday afternoon. One of the boats was heading back to port when it passed by Koroa beach. The Lions hotel was just above the beach on the headland. It was no more than 200 metres to shore, so Anton, a burly, athletic type who had played rugby well into his 40s, decided to take the plunge and swim to shore. He appeared fine, thrashing through the surf. The boats, with several Lions on board, carried on to port.

The Lions only discovered the horrible news a couple of hours later when they arrived back at the hotel. Anton had almost reached the shore when

The Lions and the NSW Country Cockatoos observe a minute's silence in memory of Anton Toia, who died the previous day.

he had a cardiac arrest. He was pulled from the water by a couple of teenage surfers who had spotted him in distress. An ambulance was called and frantic efforts made to revive him. It was to no avail. Lions doctor James Robson came rushing down from the hotel when the alarm was raised. It was all too late. Neil Back and Jonny Wilkinson, who had been jogging along the beach, came upon the horrible scene.

The tragedy had a devastating effect on the Lions camp. All planned meetings and activities were cancelled on Monday evening as everyone battled to come to terms with the news. Tributes poured in for Anton, who was married with three children. He had been a baggage master for more than a decade and knew players all around the world. So likeable and efficient was he that Scotland brought him to the UK to be in charge of their baggage operation for the 1999 World Cup. 'Anton was a very popular member of the party and had made a valuable contribution to the Lions cause,' said Donal Lenihan.

The Lions had to regroup quickly. The week could not have got off to a worse start. Sunday had begun with Lenihan and Ronan O'Gara having to head into Sydney to attend the judicial hearing on McRae. The Munster fly half gave his version of events. McRae attempted to vindicate his assault by claiming he had been provoked. He was not believed and was banned for seven weeks.

Lenihan had other matters to deal with that day. Will Greenwood and James Robson had to go by car to Coffs Harbour, a nine-hour drive, in order to call in at Gosford for an MRI scan on Greenwood's damaged ankle. He was out for at least ten days. 'I'm an eternal optimist,' said Greenwood, who had been forced off the 1997 tour with a head injury and concussion. 'At least I'm not waking up in a Bloemfontein hospital not knowing where I am.'

It was only when Robson arrived in Coffs late on Sunday evening that he was able to give a precise diagnosis of Dallaglio's knee. The England back-row man had taken another hefty blow on the

Will Greenwood's ankle injury, suffered against the NSW Waratahs, ruled him out of contention for the first Test.

The disappointment shows on the face of Lawrence Dallaglio as it is announced that his tour is over because of injury.

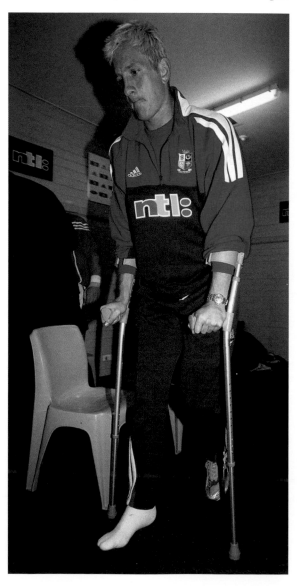

joint during the game the day before. Robson's prognosis was that Dallaglio's tour was over. There was still grave doubt too about hooker Robin McBryde. The call went out for replacements. Munster flanker David Wallace was en route to an Ireland training camp in Poland (don't ask) while Dorian West's wife thought she was about to have her husband's company in Minorca for a fortnight.

The Leicester hooker arrived there, got the message and turned straight round to head for Australia.

The pair of them arrived in Sydney at 5 a.m. on Tuesday. Ten hours later they were trotting out to their places on the Lions bench for the game against New South Wales Country Cockatoos in Coffs Harbour. 'I got the news when we stopped over at Copenhagen,' said Wallace. 'I went from there to Heathrow and on to Sydney. It's been a whirlwind. I've no idea where my luggage is, but you don't care about those things in this situation.'

The Lions had now lost five players to injury – Simon Taylor, Phil Greening, Mike Catt, Dan Luger and Lawrence Dallaglio. For Dallaglio it was the end of a frantic five-week scrap to get fit. He was downcast at not being able to push for Test selection. 'The decision to come on tour was made

with a view to completing the tour,' said Dallaglio. 'It was not made with a view to just getting a Lions shirt and then going home. I'd worked incredibly hard to get to where I was and I'm desperately disappointed that it's all ended like this. My performances, though, had not been where I expected them to be.'

Three more players were in doubt at the start of that week – Robin McBryde, Will Greenwood and Keith Wood. West's call-up was precautionary in order to spare Wood, who had a knee strain. The list of new arrivals was lengthening – Martin Corry, Gordon Bulloch, Scott Gibbs, Tyrone Howe, Dorian West and David Wallace. All of them were to play a part in the game against the Cockatoos. Iain Balshaw, who had come on tour as the form candidate for the full back spot, had been chosen for the midweek side. He had not been at his best. 'We want to give him some opportunities with ball in hand to help gain some confidence,' said Henry.

Coffs Harbour, and the match against the NSW Country Cockatoos, contrasted sharply with the Gabba four days later.

No one got much out of the match against the Cockatoos, a middling outfit not much higher up the pecking order than Western Australia. The Lions won, 46-3, but it was a flat, fractured performance. There was little spark about their play, no real drive from the forwards and precious little invention behind the scrum. All of which was a great pity for the several thousand British and Irish fans who had made the trek. The only positive performances came once again from Colin Charvis and Martin Corry in the pack. Scott Gibbs, too, packed a punch in midfield. Charvis, Gibbs, Healey, Young and Cohen scored the Lions tries. 'It was frustrating out there,' said Henry. 'It was a poor game of rugby. But we've got to box on and show strong character. It was a patchy, messy performance and we just didn't show the skill levels we ought to have done.'

Given what the squad had been through only 24 hours earlier, it was perhaps understandable that the mood was downbeat. Balshaw had been looking to press his own claims. Instead he had another mixed afternoon, trying to force the pace rather than letting the game evolve around him. It seemed that Henry was already leaning towards Matt Perry as his Test full back. 'Iain is not playing as he might,' said Henry. 'He's lacking confidence. It might only take one game to get it back. It's just a question of when that might be.'

The Wallabies would not have taken too much notice. They knew that this was the midweek side and that the Lions team to be announced on Wednesday would be quite different. The Wallabies were also in Coffs Harbour, their regular training base. They had strutted their stuff before the media on Monday lunchtime at the Pacific Bay Resort Hotel. It was all very slick, all very manicured, but you did wonder against this Stepford Wives backdrop whether all these fit, young blokes were spending too much time in camps and not enough time out there where it really mattered in the middle. 'We've only got one game under our belt and that's not normal going into matches of this standard,' said Wallaby coach Rod Macqueen. 'We know too that against the Lions we'll have to play the best football we've ever played.'

The Wallabies had made three changes to their 22-man squad. Wing Joe Roff was fit again, so too

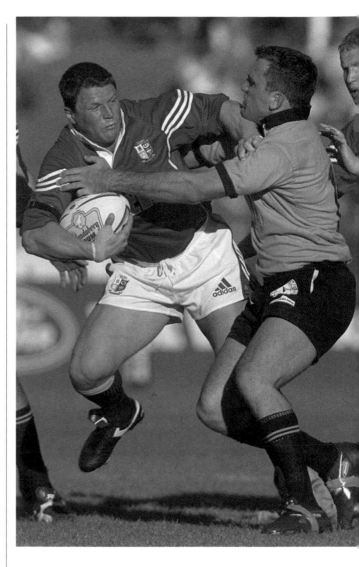

Try scorer Scott Gibbs hands off Kieran Shepherd of the Cockatoos during the 46-3 Lions victory at Coffs Harbour.

flanker Matt Cockbain, who had been hospitalised on the eve of the game against New Zealand Maori when a skin infection flared up close to his eye. Owen Finegan was recalled too after serving his five-week suspension for stamping. The Wallabies were in decent order. All that was left to do was to plot and to scheme. 'You can only speculate how the Lions might play,' said Macqueen. 'They might be holding something back for the Tests. It's impossible to tell. We'll know the idiosyncracies of

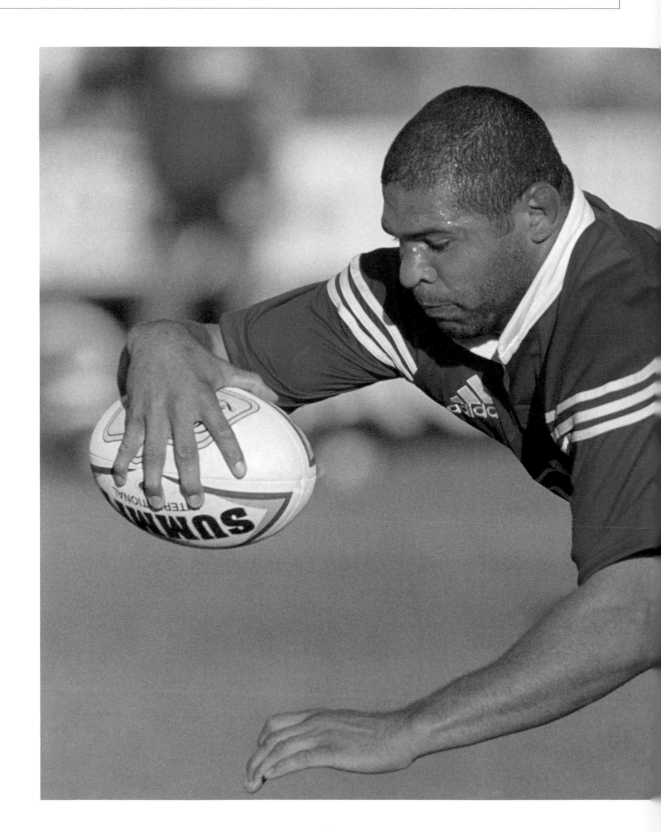

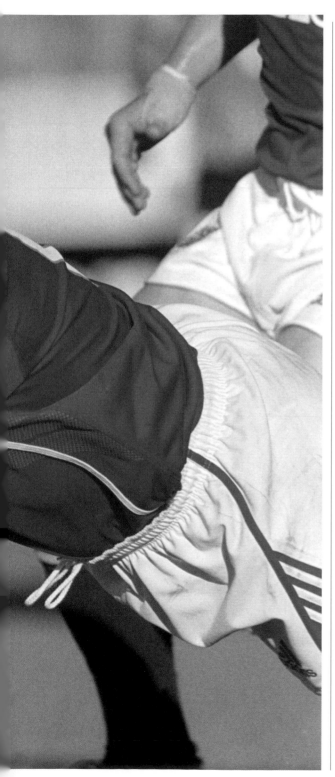

a few of their players but won't really know how they're going to put it all together.'

Macqueen had scooped the lot in his four years as Wallaby coach – World Cup, Tri-Nations and Bledisloe. He was to step aside at the end of the Australian season and hand over to Eddie Jones. The Lions scalp would be a tidy memento for the mantelpiece. 'I don't see this as a personal issue at all,' said Macqueen. 'This is all about teamwork. I'm personally excited by the challenge, but if we are to succeed it will be as a group.'

Both teams declared their hand on Wednesday. The Lions sprang a surprise when it was revealed that Neil Back had not recovered from a bang in the ribs and was not available for selection. Martin Corry completed a bewildering few weeks, going from Lions discard to Lions blind-side flanker. Perry did get the nod at full back, while Tom Smith slotted in at loose-head. Rob Henderson teamed up with Brian O'Driscoll in the centre.

It was a team forged from adverse circumstance. It was solid and efficient on paper and seemingly set on taking the game to the Wallabies through the forwards, with Henderson likely to be launched on cut-back runs from midfield. That was the theory, at least. Henry was, quite rightly, giving nothing away. 'Yes, we do have a game plan,' he said. 'And, no, I'm not going to tell you what it is. We've seen certain things with the Australians that we think we can take advantage of. The loss of certain personnel has not made any difference to the way we're going to play the game.'

Intriguing. What the hell was he on about? The media didn't know. The Wallabies probably didn't either. Just as long as the Lions players did. The game of bluff and counter-bluff has become a well-rehearsed (and tedious) feature of Test match build-up. Both teams will vie with the other for the tag of underdogs. Both will float a few notions in the media that rarely bear any resemblance to what is actually going on.

The Lions may have lost speed with Back's absence, but they gained line-out presence. That was certainly a phase of the game in which they

Colin Charvis, who once again impressed in the back row, crosses for the Lions against the Cockatoos.

Martin Johnson, Donal Lenihan and Graham Henry announce the team selected for the first Test.

Ireland that there was a touch of magic in his play, an ability to create situations from nothing. One of the wings outside him, Jason Robinson, was another master of that art. Nine months after switching codes from rugby league, Robinson was to get a start for the British Lions. It was one hell of a conversion. Robinson, a self-contained, modest bloke off the field, is a thoroughly revved-up professional sportsman, one wholly confident in his own abilities. He knew that and the opposition knew that, too.

The Wallabies, who chose Nathan Grey ahead of Elton Flatley at inside centre, had their own rugby league convert in Andrew Walker, albeit the ACT wing had played union as a schoolboy. Walker was familiar with what Robinson had to offer. 'Mate, he's a hero over here,' said Walker, who had changed codes 18 months before. 'If he walked down the street in Australia they'd all know him from what he did in league. He's electric and got all the skills in the world. Mate, he's really kicked off.'

Mate, that he has. The most impressive thing about Robinson's rise was not so much that his bewitching feet had left several would-be tacklers in his wake on the trip. No, we all knew he could do that from his time in league. But could he hit rucks and mauls when required? Could he be in the right place at the right time to lend support to a movement? Could he anticipate what was going to happen when he'd still only got 20 or so games of union under his belt?

It certainly seemed that way. 'He's a breath of fresh air, isn't he?' said Graham Henry. 'He's not bound by convention like other union players. He just does his own thing, popping up where he likes. He's been a revelation.'

The Lions management had spent a lot of time discussing the make-up of the replacements' bench, and especially just who might cover goal-kicking duties. In the end they resisted the thought of going for a specialist such as Neil Jenkins or Ronan O'Gara, opting instead for the creative mischief-making of Austin Healey. 'We decided to go down that route, figuring that Austin might just get us a couple of tries in the closing stages of a game,' said Henry. Matt Dawson and Iain Balshaw were the other substitute backs, while Jason Leonard,

could expect to give the Wallabies a hard time. For Corry, so often a benchman for England, it was a fitting reward for his honest toil and enthusiasm on tour. 'This is a huge honour,' said Corry. 'I didn't even know Backy was struggling. Coming late to the tour has taken a bit of the pressure off me. It's been a bit backs-to-the-wall for the lads. But that sort of thing tends to bring the best out of me.'

The Lions had a few trump cards that they could play. Brian O'Driscoll had shown in the colours of

Owen Finegan (No. 6) and Jeremy Paul test Nathan Grey, who was preferred to Elton Flatley in the Wallaby starting XV.

Gordon Bulloch, Colin Charvis and Martyn Williams were to cover the forward positions.

The Lions made the one-hour flight up to Brisbane late on Wednesday afternoon. There are always a few reluctant flyers in any squad. Doctor James Robson was one of them. This was his third successive Lions tour. He had been a busy man on this trip. 'I hope it eases up,' said Robson, a GP as well as a physiotherapist by training and a popular, much-respected member of the squad. 'I wouldn't mind seeing just a tiny bit of Australia rather than a hotel room or a hospital.'

The Lions were based back at the Sheraton in the centre of the city. The hotel lobby was to be a hub of activity as the thousands of fans poured into town. By the time touring teams get to their Test destination town, it's usually time to rein right back.

The hard yards have been ploughed elsewhere. Thursday is the official day off for the players, although there are always a couple of spotters ('walk through' sessions) for them to attend. The tour captain, too, might have a few official functions to perform.

Martin Johnson used to treat duties of this type with the sort of disdain a lamp post might reserve for an approaching dog. The public stage is not his favourite arena unless there are 29 other blokes there getting stuck into each other with a rugby ball in the middle. However, Johnson has both matured and mellowed, seen the bigger picture as far as obligations to the media and sponsors are concerned.

The First Test

John Eales and Martin Johnson show off the Tom Richards Cup, the trophy for which the Lions and Wallabies would compete.

Johnson could often come over as curt and gloomy. It was no more than surface appearance. On the Lions tour to South Africa in 1997 it was all part of the package, Johnson and his Lions standing up physically and mentally to all that the Springboks could throw at them. Four years later, Johnson was much more adept at the PR game. He was more relaxed with the media and more comfortable with his role. He was a good frontman, always sharp and thoughtful in his responses. There were times when he did not say very much, but that was invariably because not very much needed to be said. His insights into the game were always honest and revealing.

But the image of the beetle-browed man of silence lingered on, ready to be trotted out whenever it suited. It suited that Thursday morning at the Gabba. Johnson had agreed to do a photo shoot with his opposite number, Wallaby captain John Eales. The Tom Richards Cup had been put up for the series in memory of a great old man of Australia, whose multifaceted life has been vividly portrayed in a book by one of Australia's foremost rugby writers, Greg Growden. *Gold, Mud N'Guts* is the remarkable story of Richards, the only man ever to play for both the Wallabies and the Lions and a member of the Australian side that won gold in the 1908 Olympics. He also served right through the Gallipoli campaign in World War I and went on to win the Military Cross on the western front.

All of this would have been unknown to Johnson as he wandered along to Brisbane's famous old cricket ground that bright Thursday morning. Also unknown to him was the fact that there would be a battery of TV news crews there waiting to interview him. Or nail him. Johnson was not prepared to take the risk.

'This was supposed to be a photo shoot not a press conference,' said Johnson. He turned on his heels as the lights and microphones closed in and strolled over to the cricket square, while Eales trotted out a few lines for the cameras. One shrug from Johnson often conveys more than a hundred words from Eales.

Lions fly half Jonny Wilkinson gets in some kicking practice at the Gabba on the eve of the first Test.

Johnson was more than happy to do as scheduled, which was to pose with the trophy along with Eales. Nobody explained the purpose of promoting a match that could have sold out four times over, but that was not mentioned when the local TV networks got to work on the supposedly glum, unco-operative Johnson. Johnson was entirely in the right, but the truth of the matter was of little interest. The Lions captain was the lead item on Brisbane news bulletins, and splashed across the sports pages next day were tales of Johnson's snub. Every little dig. It's all fair game down under, mate.

Johnson might well have fancied a more leisurely tour of the Gabba. He's a sports nut, from rugby through to American Football. The Gabba,

scene of the celebrated tied Test match between Australia and the West Indies in 1960, had staged the 1950 game between the Wallabies and the Lions, won by the Lions 19-6. It had seen many great white-flannelled sportsmen walking down the pavilion steps, including one of England's finest, Ian Botham, for a season.

Even if Johnson had the inclination to browse, he had no time. The management had a chance to look around and to examine the facilities they had inspected nine months earlier on a recce trip. Surprise, surprise, the set-up had changed. 'We were told then that we would be able to use the changing rooms of the Brisbane Lions,' said Lenihan. 'Now we've been told that we can't. What's the point of me coming out in the first place if you get messed around now? The rooms are small, too small for warming up properly. You can't do that outside because there's pre-match entertainment.' There was also a bit of a fuss over the Friday training slots. The Lions had been told that they could only train at the Gabba from 9 a.m. until 10.30. The pitch would not be marked out, as there was an Australian Rules game that evening. They took their own cones along to mock up a rugby pitch and help their kickers orientate themselves on the oval.

There was also concern over the state of the turf. It was hard in the middle where it had been cut short for cricket. There was also a slight dome there as befits a cricket square. The surface had been levelled for the Olympics so that a pool stage of the soccer tournament could be played there, but the hump had then been reinstated. 'It is hard and we've spoken to the groundsman to see if it can be watered,' said Henry on Friday lunchtime. The coach was also asked to respond to claims that the Lions had been cold and unco-operative. 'Unfriendly and grumpy?' said Henry. 'What a load of rubbish. How's that for grumpiness?'

How much of all this unsettles either teams or players in the build-up? Very little. In fact most of them feed off it if they know anything about it in the first place. On an overseas tour, players very rarely tend to read too much of the local press. They might catch a headline or pick up a TV news broadcast, but they are usually very self-contained.

What they couldn't have failed to notice, however, were the gathering British and Irish hordes in the city. Brisbane was slowly being taken over, with red-clad supporters all wearing either a replica Lions shirt or fleece, the sort of outfits that you wouldn't be seen dead in back home but which were the colours of the tribe. And the tribe was going into battle.

Both teams had taken time to talk to South African referee Andre Watson. They would have put their side of events, asked for clarification on tackle and scrum, and he would have simply restated the laws as they stood in the book. Refereeing has become such a critical part of the game that some sides regard this chat as the most important part of the build-up. Quite whether it makes the slightest difference is another matter.

Watson is a vastly experienced referee. He was not the least bit fazed by all the talk of possible violence. 'If something ugly happens I'm going to deal with it,' said Watson. 'A lot of people might not like it, but it will be the thing to do. You do get this sporadic silliness. We are all human beings and we all make mistakes. Sometimes we lose our heads and this will continue to happen. We will never get rid of this. It's a contact sport. You get upset when people hit you. I'll read the moment and I should be good enough to handle it when it happens, if it happens. But I honestly don't see a problem.'

The tipsters were siding with the Wallabies. David Campese had them by ten points. Campo

Andre Watson (left), referee for the first Test, chats with Wallaby coach Rod Macqueen (right) and his assistant Ewen McKenzie.

had been featuring in a hilarious television ad for Bundaberg Rum, the sponsors of the series. The backdrop was Campo's howler in the decisive third Test against the Lions in 1989, when his badly directed pass was pounced on by Ieuan Evans, who scored. Campo was seen lobbing a can of the famous brew right past a giant white bear sitting in a chair in Campo's front room. It raised a smile, particularly in the teetotal Campese household.

More worrying matters were brewing as the Lions arrived at the Gabba that Saturday evening. Matt Dawson's *Daily Telegraph* tour diary had appeared just a couple of hours earlier in the UK. It made for a riveting read, although not a complimentary one if you were part of the Lions management sharply criticised by Dawson for being heavy handed in training.

The media were abuzz with the story, rushing around trying to get copies of exactly what had been said and wondering if the Lions themselves knew of the storm that was building. Several journalists even wondered if Dawson would actually take his place on the bench. He was there all right. The Lions knew nothing about the *Daily Telegraph* piece. They would do.

For now, though, they were all focused on what lay before them. Martin Johnson came out to toss the coin about an hour before kick-off. He couldn't believe what he saw. The stands of the Gabba were already packed with British and Irish supporters. By kick-off they numbered some 20,000 in a crowd of 37,500. It was an astonishing sight. Three Lions fans were caught on a TV news clip shouting, 'Aussie! Aussie! Aussie! Where? Where? Where?'

Rugby alone could not explain the phenomenal numbers. The figures just did not stack up. There were many factors at work, the Oz factor being one of them. It's not the worst place to visit in the world even in midwinter. There was a sense, too, that many of the fans, and they were drawn from all corners of the four countries and all classes, had come for a good time. In most countries people go to big football tournaments such as Euro 2000 or the World Cup in France in 1998 to enjoy

Jason Robinson celebrates scoring with his first touch on his Lions Test debut. Following pages: Lions fans at the Gabba.

Lions left wing Jason Robinson eludes Wallaby full back Chris Latham on his way to scoring the first Lions try at the Gabba.

themselves. The English go there to fight. Here, with the Lions, was a proper outlet for those who wanted to watch sport and to party. It was a marvellous sight.

And they got their money's worth. The start to the 2001 series was simply sensational. This is how *The Daily Telegraph* summed it up: 'There are not many Shane Warne moments in life, an instant when the heart skips and a wonderful new sporting reality takes shape. The blond spinner did it with his first ball against Mike Gatting eight years ago; Jason Robinson managed it with his first touch as a Lion on Saturday evening in Brisbane. The Wallabies, cocksure world champions, were so certain of themselves that their full-back Chris Latham had the brass neck to show the Lions winger the outside line in the third minute confident that he would smash him into touch. Robinson took it, skated past and the ego of an entire sporting nation was dealt a devastating blow.

Jonny Wilkinson offloads to Rob Henderson as George Smith makes the tackle. Keith Wood, as usual, is on the spot to help.

'These were not just rugby's Wallabies that were being humiliated. These were Australia's Wallabies, the land of Olympic gold and brazen self-belief, the country for whom sport is a barometer of national well-being. A deep depression has settled across the nation.

'It was not just the victory that triggered the Aussie blues, it was the manner of it. It was one of the greatest Lions performances of all time. Robinson's cameo was just the start of it. It doesn't take much for an Australian to sneer at his stuffy, hidebound, timid cousins from the Mother Country. Mate, no soul and no sense of adventure. On Saturday the men from the four home unions played like new world pioneers. From the moment

Willie John McBride gave an emotional rallying speech when handing out the shirts in the team room at the hotel beforehand the Lions were forthright and positive, not cowed or overawed by their circumstance or by the opposition.'

The Lions were bold and brazen, playing intense football right across the field. The Wallabies were caught in the spotlights. They were visibly taken aback by the pace of the Lions game as well as by their upbeat attitude. The fact that there were 20,000 voices roaring support up in the stands only added to the torment.

All the positive plays in that opening quarter came from the Lions. The Wallabies were rattled. Latham dropped a high ball, fly half Stephen Larkham was slow to respond and was wrapped in a great bear-hug tackle by Keith Wood and Martin Johnson. They turned over ball in midfield as the

Lions piled in. Rob Henderson made a sharp break only to be intercepted by Joe Roff with Brian O'Driscoll clear outside. It was breathless stuff.

The tension refused to ease. In the 15th minute the Lions laid down a series of scrums on the Wallaby line. The Australian pack creaked and was in trouble. The Lions got the nudge on only for the Wallaby scrum half to kick the ball out of the Lions back row. Penalty. Gregan was lucky that it was not a yellow card and a penalty try. The Lions went again. The Wallaby scrum wobbled. Down it went. Again the Lions scrummed hard, but this time Rob Howley went for the break, fed Scott Quinnell who was brought down. Pile-up, penalty to Australia.

An opportunity wasted? Certainly. Was the tide turning? Perhaps. A few minutes later Dafydd James was nailed coming out of defence by Gregan. The Lions came in from the side – penalty to the Wallabies, which Andrew Walker put between the posts. Twenty-two minutes gone, 5-3 to the Lions.

That was as good as it got for the Wallabies until the 76th minute, by which time the Lions were well and truly in the driving seat at 29-3. The Wallabies disappeared from sight, hanging on for dear life as the Lions split them fore and aft. Johnson and Grewcock swamped them in the line out, Corry doing his bit too. Keith Wood was a monumental presence, in body and soul. His warrior spirit, the raging physicality of his play, spurred on his red-shirted mates. Wallaby centre Nathan Grey was flattened by one huge hit in the 33rd minute.

Somehow the Wallabies were holding their try line. Something had to give. It duly did either side

Australia scrum half George Gregan exhorts his forwards to greater effort, but it was not to be the Wallabies' night.

Brian O'Driscoll lights up the Gabba by running home from halfway. Joe Roff catches him on the line – but too late.

of half-time, with Brian O'Driscoll playing a prominent part in the action. His low-slung break down the blind side in the 39th minute, heading through flanker Owen Finegan, carved up the Wallaby defence. Jason Robinson had read the play superbly, coming off his wing and sweeping round to provide the link for Dafydd James to score.

Less than a minute into the second half O'Driscoll did it all himself, slipping between Grey and Jeremy Paul and spearing downfield. Matt Burke had raced up from full back to try and put pressure on the Irishman. It was the only ploy left to Burke. It didn't even register with O'Driscoll who left one of the most experienced full backs in the world flat on his rear end. It was a sensational try.

The stadium erupted. The meanest defence in the world, which had conceded only one try during the entire 1999 World Cup, were being made to look like novices, very startled novices at that.

The theoretical second-half revival by the Wallabies, the moment when teams come back after a rousing half-time pep talk, when the momentum shifts from one side to the other, had been stopped in its tracks. The Wallabies were not going anywhere. The force was still with the Lions.

The Lions were declaring their hand, defining themselves, for themselves as much as for the millions watching. This was the time that they truly came together, found out what each other was made of and what they were made of collectively. It was a gripping spectacle in all aspects.

Wilkinson kicked a goal five minutes later and the Lions were heading towards the horizon. They were over it seven minutes later when Scott Quinnell plunged through to touch down for the fourth Lions try. Henderson had triggered the move, breaking the tackle and heading deep into Wallaby territory. He was eventually hauled down, but Rob Howley and Iain Balshaw, who had come on at half-time for the injured Matt Perry, took it on. Another desperate lunge by the Wallaby defence, another pile-up. Quinnell arrived, got his hands on the ball and blasted through. Wilkinson's conversion made it 29-3 with 55 minutes gone. The Wallabies were obliterated.

Sure, they did come back as the Lions took their foot off the pedal, anxious not to make mistakes with such a big lead. Of course mistakes are exactly what they did make with such an attitude. It was inevitable, too, that the world champions would have their moments. Video referee Kelvin Deaker

ruled on an effort by Matt Burke in the 61st minute which went the way of the Lions. The Wallabies were beginning to build some phase play. The Lions were forced on to the back foot. In the 69th minute the first crack appeared when Martin Corry was sin-binned for persistent infringement.

The Wallabies accepted their opportunity. They found a bit of space in the 76th minute and Walker took full advantage, cutting infield past Phil Vickery and then stepping Balshaw. Three minutes later the Lions were breached on the other side of the field after the Wallabies had successfully put together half a dozen phases. This time is was Grey who finished it off, Joe Roff pulling the cover across before feeding inside to his centre.

Scott Quinnell pauses for thought after bursting through from close range to score the fourth Lions try.

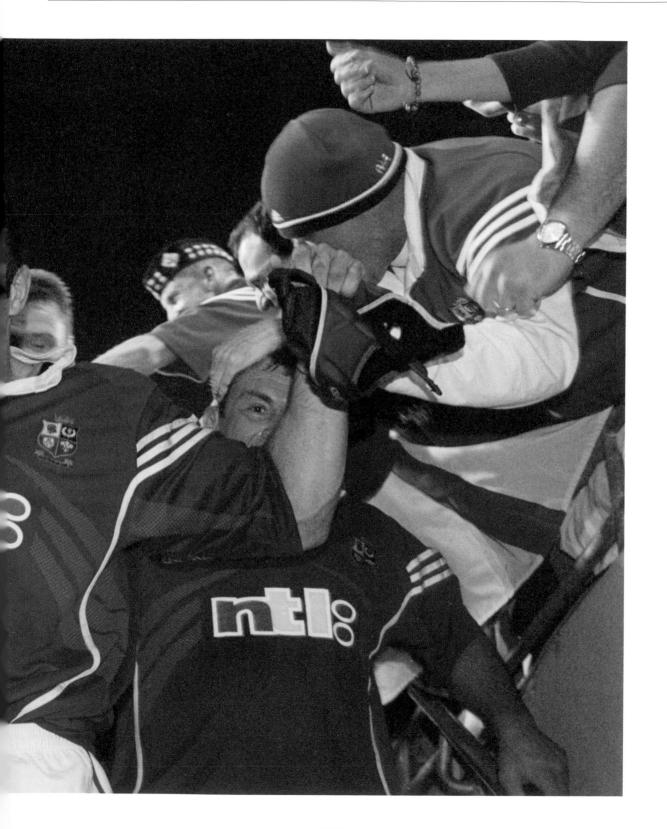

Graham Henry and Andy Robinson share the victory. Previous pages: Lions fans salute their heroes as they leave the field.

Two tries had been scored with Corry off the field. The Lions were to lose Vickery in the 85th minute, the tight-head also adjudged to have been persistently trying to slow down the ball. By then, though, the day was done for the Wallabies. Up in the stands wave after wave of song – 'Bread of Heaven', 'Molly Malone' interspersed with a few 'Chariots' – rolled round the Gabba. Watson blew his final whistle and the stadium erupted.

It had been a hammer blow victory. The Wallabies had been damn near humiliated. The Lions had lifted themselves from the low of the build-up to hit an unbelievable height of performance. Whatever was to happen from here on in, they had proved themselves as an outstanding bunch of individuals and, most significantly, as a team with a strong nerve and iron character. To the fore as ever was Martin Johnson.

Not for him a self-indulgent revel in the moment. No, a few words for the flash TV interviews, a quick, yet sincere wave to the adoring and demented thousands, and a turn on the heel and down the tunnel. Not for him a lap of honour. He knew that the job was not even half done. Winning a Test match is one thing. Winning a series is quite another. He knew that the Wallabies would regroup. Little did he realise as he headed towards the dressing room that the Lions would have to do their own regrouping. The faxes and e-mails from London were already red hot with tales of Dawson's revelations.

There was no such thing as a lull on this Lions tour. This extraordinary tale took another twist.

TRUE

PERFORMANCE
Jason Robinson

TISSOT

passenger request: *Spoil me*

Delta BusinessElite®:

5 courses of tasty things to eat
a fine wine (or two)
all the films you've been meaning to see, TV and your kind of music
a serve yourself snack table
ice-cream sundaes so huge they're sinful

▲Delta

fly 5-Star

www.delta.com

Match views: First Test

Graham Henry

The Lions and Wallaby media had been calling him 'Grumpy' Graham Henry. But if there is a dictionary definition of 'ungrumpiness' it was written in big headlines on the coach's face when he met the press after the first Test. He did his best not to gloat over Australia or patronise them – but it was not easy. His smirk was as wide as Sydney Harbour:

'We are massively elated, having played pretty good rugby for most of the game. The players showed huge amounts of character after our difficult week internally. But it's feet-on-the-ground time. That was not a one-off Test, and if we play like that last 25 minutes when we face the wounded Wallaby next week in Melbourne we will get smashed.'

The Irish midfield duo of Brian O'Driscoll (No. 13) and Rob Henderson celebrate at no-side.

Then it was time to praise famous men:

'Brian O'Driscoll was supreme. He is electric with the ball, but don't forget his centre partner, Rob Henderson, who did a lot of talking and was a mature presence in midfield. Jonny Wilkinson was immense – and think how young he is. And Jason Robinson. He just loves playing rugby of any sort, getting out there and expressing himself through whatever code he chooses.'

Donal Lenihan

Henry nominated 'the driving line outs' as the outstanding factor in a pragmatic display by the pack, and it was left to Donal Lenihan, the Lions manager from Munster, to single out another Munsterman:

'Keith Wood had been promising to land a drop goal in a Test and his multi-skills as a hooker who is everywhere enabled him to get not too far short with that drop kick from near halfway.'

Martin Johnson

Captain Martin Johnson was asked to toss the coin in public for the benefit of TV, and when he went back into the dressing room he said:

'Lads, it's a home game for us because there are so many red-shirted fans here and they are already making an incredible noise.'

Johnson, as a player, has beaten all the Lions' opponents in the last eight years. New Zealand in Wellington in 1993, then as captain in the series victory in South Africa in 1997 and now the happy hat-trick. He is also a virtually invincible leader back home. Still, he insisted:

'This was one of the greatest Test performances I have been involved in. We have been on the go for almost 11 months since picking ourselves up for the start of the last European season, and there have been grumbles within this squad. We have been in Australia a long time and endured some tough times. But a convincing result like this makes all the effort and sacrifice worthwhile.'

Brian O'Driscoll

O'Driscoll, who provided the moment of the match with his try straight after the interval, confessed that he was surprised that the Wallaby defence proved so vulnerable:

'Their defensive record was so good in World Cup 99 and has been so hyped during this tour that when we broke it comfortably early on with Jason Robinson's try our self-belief grew. We became unafraid to try things. My try was donated by Jonny Wilkinson. There were a couple of forwards hanging around in the Australian back line and I "shouldered" them off and had the gas to beat the last tackler.'

Richard Hill

Flanker Richard Hill, a grafter and a shrewd reader of the game, said:

'The flood of penalties we gave away in the second half were difficult to understand.'

But he and the Lions hardly cared about the penalties and the yellow cards.

Rod Macqueen

Australia's coach took the defeat with dignity but needed to save face with a couple of stiletto words:

'They made us pay for every mistake with intelligent but conservative rugby.'

Conservative! Four tries! I think that Tory leader William Hague would have settled for the political equivalent of four tries in the June 2001 election.

Macqueen was realistic when he noted:

'They cut us to bits down the middle. Our passion was there, but not the skill when it mattered.'

John Eales

Australia's distinguished captain commented:

'We need to emulate exactly what the Lions did in 1989 here, when they hit back from a first-Test hammering to win the series 2-1.'

Rob Howley

And Lions scrum half Rob Howley confirmed the importance of the first score:

'We knew that if we could get in behind them once, we could manage to break them again.'

Later in an evening when the Lions and their supporters again attacked the world celebrating record, Howley revealed that the Lions match-shirts had been presented by Willie John McBride, a five-times Lion and captain of the victorious squad in South Africa in 1974:

'It was a master stroke to bring in Willie John. We are far from his generation, but we all know that he is a symbol of the Lions tradition. He made a stirring speech about the past and the glory that awaited us and there was emotion and weeping among the squad. Tears of joy later, though!'

Rob Howley and Scott Quinnell reflect on the evening's events, another extraordinary chapter in Lions history.

Reflections: First Test

COMMENTS FROM THE LIONS COACH
Graham Henry in conversation with Ian Robertson

When the Lions assembled in the UK at the end of May you must have had some idea of what your probable Test team would be. How different was that embryo side from the team actually selected for the first Test?
I think there were probably about four or five changes. There were some people we picked whose form hasn't been as good as we had hoped and other players who have surprised us and whose form has been excellent. From the team that we had in the back of our minds before we left the UK, I think that about a third of those players have fallen by the wayside either through injury or loss of form.

How difficult has it been for you to pull four different countries together and then select a team and blend them into a unit in five weeks? Has it been quite straightforward?
No, it hasn't been straightforward. The biggest challenge I've had is to share the coaching duties with a number of other people. I've coached for some years now and usually I've coached by myself or with one assistant forwards coach, whereas here I have been coaching with several quality coaches and I've got a huge amount of time for them. It's been great to work with people like Andy Robinson, Phil Larder, Steve Black, Dave Alred and the video analysis guys, but I've had to change the way I've coached. I have been used to being in sole charge and I have had to adjust to this new and very different role. I wasn't sure for a long time whether I was doing the right thing. I knew after the first Test that it was the right way, but it was foreign to me and I found that quite difficult at first.

How did you choose the tactics for the Test? Was it your decision or did every coach have a voice?
No, the tactics to use against Australia were something we've been working on for 12 months.

There has been a huge amount of research on how the Australians play, their individual players, any perceived weaknesses we thought we could take advantage of. So that has been an ongoing process that started last year in August, September, October, before we got involved in the Six Nations as coaches. I did a lot of research on the Australians and so did the other coaches as well, so we came away from Tylney Hall that first week together in the UK in May with a game plan in mind to attack what we saw as some Australian weaknesses.

In the first Test we saw possibly the best 60 minutes of rugby in the last 20 years from the Lions. Where did you think the key areas were in the Lions performance which won the Test for you?
I think our defence was outstanding and I think our defence right through the tour has been generally pretty good. I think Phil Larder's done a superb job there and I think it shows the character of the team. If you haven't got that, you have got nothing to build on. I think you've got to start with a very strong foundation defensively and I think this side has that strong foundation. The second thing is that we were bold. We took the Australians on with the ball and if we're going to beat the Australians we've got to continue to be bold.

The physical aspect of the forward battle went 100 per cent the Lions way in the first hour. Did it surprise you that the Australians didn't put up more resistance, and secondly do you think they were perhaps a little overconfident and complacent going into that match as all the talk had been of them winning by 15-20 points?
I think they were concerned initially on the tour after our performance against Queensland. There was a lot of propaganda going on in the newspapers and through the media. I think they tried to break up the rhythm of the tour and our concentration on what we were trying to do. I think they wanted us to revert back to playing a tight game, to take them on as a forward pack and play

percentage rugby with a lot of driving and kicking. I'm just pleased that we didn't fall into that trap. We were not at our best in the two games immediately prior to the Test, against Australia A and New South Wales, which I think probably gave the Australians a lot more confidence than they would have had after the Queensland game. Also, I think they were underdone. A lot of those guys hadn't played for five weeks and I know that even though we're playing far too much rugby at the moment, generally speaking, five weeks before a Test match of that magnitude they were a little rusty and not quite up to speed. And in the first 20 minutes I think that gave us an edge. It won't happen in the second Test. They've got that game under their belt now. They went in underprepared and perhaps a

The Wallabies came unstuck in Brisbane, but the Lions coach was under no illusions about what to expect in Melbourne.

little overconfident in Brisbane. It will be completely different in Melbourne. You also have to remember our guys played particularly well for the first 60 minutes of the game.

How can you explain the sudden turnaround from attacking and running them ragged for nearly an hour to spending the last 20 minutes in your own half defending? Did you say to the team, 'Now let them have the ball and we'll practise our defence

ready for the second Test', which would be a brilliant coaching coup if that's what you did?
It's exactly what we did, of course.

Now tell us what really went wrong in the last 20 minutes.
We had played so well to lead 29-3 that I think the guys thought that that was it, the game had been won and they switched off a bit. We discussed it afterwards and the feeling was we got conservative, we didn't maintain our boldness, so we kicked the ball back to them. We tried to play safety first and what we were really doing was giving them an opportunity to get back into the game. We kicked the ball from first phase which we shouldn't have done. We should have built our game and built it so that we could play it down their end. We have to admit we were disappointing in the last 20 minutes.

Do you think it's been a huge plus for you that you had that very sticky final 20 minutes because that will help to focus the guys' minds for the second Test?
I think it's going to be helpful, but I think we need more than that. There's a lot of turnarounds in rugby as you'll remember from the 1997 Lions tour and the 1989 tour, where they got beaten by a big score in the first Test and turned it around in the second. There are a lot of examples of that and I think our guys have got to be very wary of that sort of thing. The Australians are going to be the best that they can be on Saturday in Melbourne. Psychologically they're going to be right on the button. I'd imagine they'll use little kicks in behind our defensive pattern. We've just got to make sure we build correctly because I still think we've got quite a few irons in the fire that we haven't shown yet. I think we were playing at only 80 per cent of our full capacity in that first 60 minutes in Brisbane. I think we can play better than we played in the first Test match and that must be the goal.

As a one-off match, would the first-Test win be the highlight of your career thus far, or not?
I don't really think of it in that way because it is not about individuals it is about the squad. But having said that, there was a huge amount of personal satisfaction in winning the first Test.

FROM AN AUSTRALIAN VIEWPOINT
by MICHAEL LYNAGH

What an extraordinary game! The Lions played better than anybody expected. They really hadn't given any indication in the lead-up to the first Test that they were capable of playing that well. Sure, we all knew that they were individually great players and that if it all came together on the night they would be very hard to beat, but we didn't realise just what they were capable of.

The Wallabies suffered from shell shock in the first 20 minutes as the Lions hit them with everything but the kitchen sink. A lot of the Wallaby players hadn't played any rugby for three weeks or longer and when the Lions started the game at such pace and using the width of the field the Australians were caught out.

Jason Robinson scored the first try, and all that did was to confirm with the Lions team that more of the same was needed. It gave them the confidence and impetus to continue with the barrage. On the other hand, the Wallabies, who in the past, when the occasion warranted it, have been able to up the tempo a notch or two, were struggling to get out of second gear.

The Lions defence was awesome. They continually knocked over the Wallabies go-forward men, Finegan and Kefu. This then didn't allow the ball players, namely Larkham and Gregan, any room or momentum to use their skills. The Lions attack, on the other hand, was well organised and potent. They didn't just attack in one area or in one way, they varied it very well. They were managing to break through the Aussie defence – something a lot of other teams haven't been able to do. The centres, Henderson and ODriscoll, were simply outstanding. They were a threat to the Wallabies every time they touched the ball. Their defence in tandem with Jonny Wilkinson was rock solid.

There was no area of the game in which Australia could say that they were dominant. The Lions won in every area of the match. The only worry for the Lions, and a glimmer of hope for the wounded Wallabies, was the last 20 minutes of the match. With the game won, the Lions seemed to retreat into defending a lead, whereas the Wallaby machine slowly started to rumble into some sort of rhythm. Both Graham Henry and Martin Johnson talked about this after match, and I am sure that if the Lions are in a similar position again, then they will continue to attack the win rather than try to hold onto a lead.

The Wallabies will be so much better next week for this loss. They have very rarely played poorly for two games in a row. There were things such as the defensive lapses in midfield that I don't see happening again. Individually, there were some stars in the Australian team who were unusually quiet in this game. I expect to see some big games from the likes of Larkham, Eales, Gregan and Roff, who have never really let Australia down when they were needed to pull something out of nothing to win a game. The Wallabies will be much better in the second Test, but they will have to be, as this first Test match belonged to the Lions.

Wallaby fly half Stephen Larkham is closed down by marauding Lions, including Martin Johnson and Danny Grewcock.

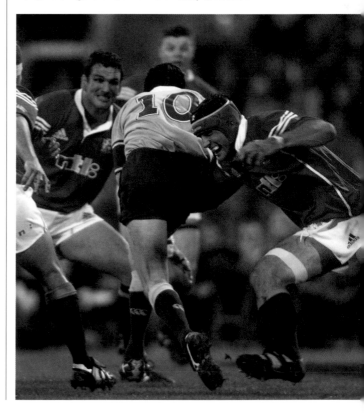

Six steps to the perfe[ct] Gordon's and toni[c]

1. Take a tall clean glass

2. Fill the glass 2/3 with ice

3. Pour Gordon's over ice

4. Top up with freshly opened premium tonic

5. Run a wedge of fresh lim[e] around the rim of the gla[ss]

6. Add the lime to the glas[s] and stir

Gordon's Gin

5. The Second Test

Matt Dawson – Judas or soul-searching, honest individual? The scrum half's whistle-blowing activities were the talk of the town. Every town. The astonishing victory of the Lions quite rightly made sporting headlines across the land. Dawson's comments made front-page news as well.

His tour diary, outlining with extraordinary candour his feelings and mood across the first four weeks of the tour made for compelling reading. He upbraided the management for beasting the players in training, flogging them from dawn to dusk. As much as he was critical of the quantity of training, Dawson was also unimpressed with the quality of

Wallaby left wing Joe Roff touches down for his second try in the second Test at the Colonial Stadium, Melbourne.

it. 'Not on same wavelength at the moment,' read his entry for Sunday 10 June. 'Andy Robinson and Phil Larder seem to be more distant than in an England context. Players are getting cheesed off with them.'

A week later, Dawson's gloom had deepened.

Monday 18 June
'We all understood that there was a lot to get through but we are wasting energy. Spend too much time on set-piece and not enough to reacting

Scrum half Matt Dawson trains with the squad after revealing that all was not as it could have been in the Lions camp.

---

to what's in front of us... everyone too bogged down by calls.'

The lid was lifted three days later.

Thursday 21 June
'It's official – some of the boys have decided to leave the tour. We said at Tylney that if this should happen we would implement peer pressure but to

be quite frank with so many young players it is hard to avoid.'

The diary was a devastating indictment of the way the tour was being run. Whether it was all true, or even partially so, was quite another matter. It was Dawson's take on events, and a brazen take it was too. He was to take an enormous amount of stick for what he had said and the timing of it on the morning of the first Test.

The timing was not the issue it appeared, seemingly more significant and calculating than it was ever likely to be. Given the nine-hour time difference, there was little chance of any news reaching the Lions camp before they set out for the match itself. And even if a snippet did reach their ears it would have nothing like the impact it would have done if it had dropped on their breakfast tables back home in Britain or Ireland.

Quite whether he should have lifted the lid on all that was going on is the only issue. Many felt that he had broken the unwritten rule that 'what goes on tour stays on tour'. The line was that he had betrayed his colleagues, let down his mates and run the serious risk of destabilising the whole tour. There is merit in that. But Dawson was not out

The Lions train in Canberra. The tour workload had been heavy. Too heavy, or at the level required to knit the side together?

The timing of the publication of the diary had nothing to do with Dawson. He had been asked before the tour began if he would be prepared to do a diary piece for a four-page supplement backed by Zurich, one of the Lions sponsors. That supplement was ordered by Zurich and booked to appear on the day of the Brisbane Test. Dawson had not manipulated it to that end. He could not have asked for the piece to be held until the Monday pages because there would not have been the space for it.

of step with several players on tour. His mood and his perspective were not unique to him. He was expressing a certain reality of the tour.

Purely in a professional sense, he ought to have kept his thoughts to himself. He was contracted to do a job and all that that job entailed. He was an employee and should have put up with whatever hardships came his way. It was a breach of

Martin Johnson affirmed that Dawson and the squad had made their peace. 'Now we just move on,' said the skipper.

confidence, contractual as well as symbolic, to do otherwise. But it was humbug to suggest that he was a traitor to the cause. That much was seen in the way that the Lions responded to his situation. Publicly they handled the matter very well. There was even a tacit acknowledgement that it had been a strenuous few weeks and that maybe, just maybe, too much had been asked of the players. The management decided on a strategy to deal with the hot issue and stuck to it. They expressed their disapproval but were not going to be drawn into wholesale, hot-tempered response.

'I was disappointed to read the comments,' said manager Donal Lenihan Sunday lunchtime. 'It is a difficult situation and I have to admit that there has been some frustration over the last few weeks. The workload has been heavy but you saw the benefits of that last night. You can't knit a side together unless you work hard. The players have not had the opportunity to let their hair down and so tensions build. We put our hands up on that one. We have also prioritised the Test team to the possible detriment of the midweek boys. It is at times difficult to keep the balance. A number of the squad are disappointed with what Matt has come out with. You might feel that he's let himself down. He has come to see me and apologised to me as well as to the coaches in person. But this has now become an internal matter and we will deal with it in house.'

It was a good performance by Lenihan. There was the right mix: of indignation yet empathy for the situation of the tour party. In private, he probably blew a gasket. In public, he did not want to give the Australians the smallest crumb of comfort. If Dawson had been sent home on the dubious grounds of 'bringing the game into disrepute', then it would have handed back so much of the initiative to the Australian camp.

It would have been the wrong course of action for other reasons. If Dawson had been bumped from the trip, there was no guarantee that one or two others might not have taken themselves with him; unlikely but possible. That too would have had a crushing impact on morale. The course the management steered was the right one. That much became clear in the next couple of days.

Dawson was given more support from a significant quarter – Martin Johnson. He had no time for the hang-him-high brigade. 'The squad made peace with Matt and Matt has made peace with the squad. Now we just move on,' said Johnson. 'Things like this in the heat of the tour are just a minor hiccup, not a major problem. I can sympathise with him. It's been an incredibly tough tour and we've all been through the mill. But he is sorry and there is no point in flogging Matt and hanging him out to dry. He feels bad enough.'

Dawson himself was taken aback by the reaction to what he had written. He had made an error of judgment; not that he backed off too much from the substance of his comments. 'It was an extraordinary weekend,' he said. 'I experienced the great high of being part of a Lions squad that beat the world champions but then had to contend with the great low of seeing the reaction to the article I had written and cope with the realisation of what I had done. I was disappointed in myself for taking the gloss off what had been a fantastic evening for all concerned. I let myself down but more importantly I let the squad down.

'There were things that were mentioned in the diary that should have remained confidential. I put in jeopardy the trust and confidence that had built up within the whole group. That means a hell of a lot to me. What makes me really tick is the sense of being part of a group. I like to be liked and I like to give my all to those around me. That was put under strain and I'm disappointed it came to that.'

Dawson had an immediate opportunity to make amends. He was chosen to play against ACT Brumbies on Tuesday evening at the Bruce Stadium in Canberra, the Milton Keynes of Australia, a contrived, concrete, purpose-built city constructed in the 1920s as the neutral capital. Canberra means 'meeting place' in Aborigine, the coming together of the one nation after the federal states of New South Wales, Victoria, Queensland and the rest decided to throw in their lot under one banner.

The city does not have a lot to recommend it. It does have one of the most evocative war memorials and museums many of us have come across, a splendid monument to the war dead of every campaign ever fought by Australian servicemen and women around the world. It all amounted to much more than a mere military exhibition. It captured the essence of the Aussie character, particularly as seen in the ill-fated

The management handled the affair sensibly, but 'there was a real sense, post-Dawson, of Henry asserting his authority'.

99

Austin Healey receives a stern rebuke from lock Justin Harrison after scoring his interception try against the Brumbies.

Gallipoli campaign in World War I. The eight-month nightmare summed up the Australian (and New Zealand) virtues of fortitude and resilience. Not many other nations would have the deep sense of self-worth to actually celebrate military failure, but that's the Aussies for you – proud of their own whatever the circumstances.

The Canberra folk were proud of their rugby team, the ACT Brumbies, Super-12 champions, the first team outside of New Zealand to take the title. They were the newcomers of the Australian provincial scene, moving in on the turf of the NSW Waratahs and Queensland Reds. And how!

The Brumbies were not, however, to give us their finest. They had a dozen players out of action with either the Wallabies or through injury. However, as is the wont of coach Eddie Jones, they were not taking this game lightly. Far from it. They had spent ten days doing the hard yards down in New Zealand, where they'd had a two-match tour, beating North Harbour but losing to Southland.

Even though it was effectively a second-string line-up, the Brumbies were certain to be well drilled and committed. Former man of Leicester (and, of course, ACT) Pat Howard was at fly half against some of his old Tigers mockers. Raw-boned lock Justin Harrison, one of the outstanding figures of the Super-12 campaign, was at the heart of the pack, and the team was to be led on the night by No. 8 Jim Williams, playing his last game for the side before heading overseas to Munster. Graeme Bond and James Holbeck in the Brumbies midfield were both quality centres.

The Lions were now into midweek mode with their side. Iain Balshaw was again at full back while Martin Corry was to play his third game in seven days, suggesting that Neil Back would be fit for Test duty the following Saturday. Corry's selection was also due to the unavailability of Colin Charvis, who was beginning a two-match suspension.

This looked like being the last game on tour for several of these 'dirt trackers'. The trip still had two weeks to run. Any thoughts of sending a few players back to base? 'No,' said Graham Henry. 'We chose 37 players for the tour and all 37 will stay to the end. A tour is a tour. That was all decided down to the last detail many months ago. We're not about to have people buggering off home.'

There was a real sense, post-Dawson, of Henry asserting his authority. Fair enough. He was the guv'nor and needed to send out the right signals. Dawson himself managed to do his own semaphore job in an extraordinary match in Canberra that Tuesday evening. Once again there was a very healthy crowd, 20,093, who were treated to a rare old scrap.

There was a great contrast in styles: the Brumbies sharp and co-ordinated against a Lions team lacking in shape and organisation and forced to rely on individual guts and brilliance to see it through. Austin Healey almost single-handedly kept his side in the hunt after they had fallen 14-0 behind within 11 minutes of the start.

I once wrote that Healey was 'an irritating little bugger' and received one of the most abusive letters I've ever had, penned in perfect script from a female Healey admirer, upbraiding me for being so patronising. So here we go again. Healey is an irritating little bugger, the perfect character you need when times are hard, on and off the field. He

Healey crosses deep in injury time against the Brumbies to tie the scores 28-28 with just the conversion to come before no-side.

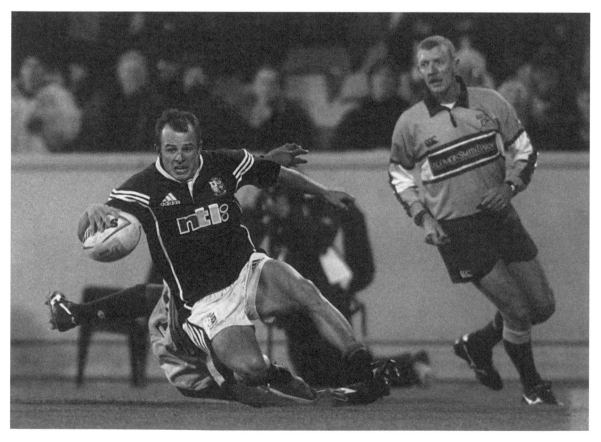

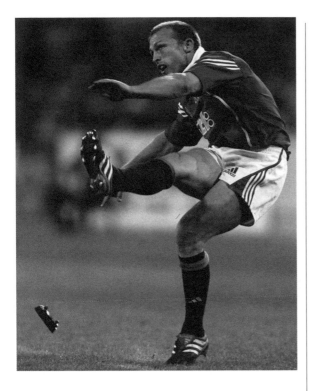

In a Boy's Own conclusion in Canberra, Dawson becomes the hero by winning the ACT game with the very last kick.

The scores were tied 28-28. Healey had faith in his soulmate, Matt Dawson, landing the conversion, even though Dawson had missed two relatively straightforward pots at goal in the second half.

The kick was just over halfway out to the touch line. It was not the most difficult in the world. Until, that is, you factor in that it was literally the last kick of the match, that Dawson had put himself through the emotional mincer with his paper talk and that he had slumped to the ground as Healey crossed for his try. Apart from that, he was in great shape.

Dawson lined it up, took his Alredesque deep breaths and smacked it straight between the posts. The Lions had won a gripping encounter, 30-28. The whistle blew and Dawson turned to the crowd clutching his Lions badge. He was swamped by his team-mates as well as by the Test squad, who had come down from their seats in the stands to cheer on their pals. It was a stirring scene, quite at odds with any notion that Dawson might have been cold-shouldered by the squad for breaking ranks.

In the dressing-room it all got the better of him and he broke down. 'The win was a big moment for everyone,' said Dawson. 'I personally got very emotional, but I think there were many others who felt likewise. The conversion was like a pressure valve being released. It blew out all the emotions of the previous few days. I did break down in the dressing room, reflecting on all the negatives of the preceding 72 hours. Dai Young and Scott Gibbs had given a very important and passionate talk at half-time, reminding us all what it meant to wear the Lions jersey. There was 40 minutes left for me to make amends.

'I was so glad to be actually playing. If I'd not been involved my head would have been all over the place. It was a pressure game and a pressure kick. But knowing myself as I do, I do like to accept challenges although I certainly wouldn't want to re-create the circumstances.

'When Austin Healey scored in the last second, I dropped to my knees. I was completely gone. The doctor rushed on to see if I was all right. I just

refuses to bow before either convention or circumstance. He will front up, whatever the odds against him. He is brave and supremely talented as well. He is also hugely irritating to the opposition.

Healey prompted so much of the Lions fightback, even though he was out on the wing. He had a running slanging match with Harrison, not the opponent you might select if you had any inkling for self-preservation. And he did the business in proper fashion too, snatching an interception try just before half-time. Healey impudently wagged his finger behind him as he raced home from halfway, taunting the opposition. Harrison took exception and chased him down to the posts to remind him that he might well have scored a try but the Lions were still trailing, 19-8.

Just over 40 minutes later it was Healey who was reminding Harrison that he had just scored his second try and that the Brumbies were about to lose. Healey's try was scored in the ninth minute of injury time, after the match hooter had sounded.

Lions prop Phil Vickery meets actress Katie Keltie, aka Michelle Scully, on a pre-Test visit to the set of the TV soap *Neighbours*.

selection. The Lions stated that they would declare their final line-up on Friday afternoon. However, little did they realise (or did they and were just playing silly buggers?) that all international line-ups had to be finalised 48 hours before kick-off – that is, by 7 p.m. Thursday.

'There is no question that this ruling does not apply,' said an International Board spokesman. And what if it were contravened? 'Well, we'd have to convene a meeting of the board to decide what sanctions we might take,' said the spokesman.

Prevent them playing the match? Scrap the next Lions tour? I don't think so. The Lions might have been trying to throw a curve ball the way of Wallaby

needed time. I realised that this was a great opportunity to put some things to rights. I cleared my head and went through all the routines I'd spent hours and hours doing on the training field with Dave Alred. I blocked it all out and let rip. It was a good contact and a good feeling.'

There was a good feeling going into the second Test. The squad made the short hop down to Melbourne the following afternoon. The team had been due to be announced that lunchtime. It was delayed, the Lions naming a squad of 27 players instead. They reasoned that they still had a few bumps and bruises to sort out and did not want to name a team only to be perhaps forced into changing it. Matt Perry was still doubtful with his groin strain, although Back was available for

Stephen Larkham felt the Wallaby game plan at the Gabba 'didn't allow myself or the rest of the team to really get into the game'.

The scene is set at the Colonial Stadium, Melbourne. Keen not to be 'out-coloured' by Lions fans, the ARU didn't stint on the gold.

coach Rod Macqueen. That's how ARU managing director John O'Neill saw it. 'It appears to be game-playing,' he said. 'The fact of the matter is that there are regulations that have to be complied with.'

If the intention was to cause minor irritation in the Wallaby camp, then the Wallaby camp did not appear to be playing ball. 'We are so much concerned with ourselves at the moment that it's just not an issue,' said Macqueen. 'We're too busy trying to get our own act together. I don't know whether they're playing mind games or not. It certainly doesn't affect us, the situation we're in at the moment. At another time it might have been a bigger issue.'

The Lions came clean on Thursday evening, falling into line with IB regulations. There was no great surprise about the side – Back was in, Corry was out and Perry was fit. 'Neil was going to start

in the first Test, so we've just gone with what we had always intended,' said Henry. 'He's a very important part of the back-row unit. He gives us width and continuity and acts as defensive captain.' Even so, it was tough on Corry, a real trouper.

The Lions were in confident mood. They sensed that the force was with them. The Australians had even begun to question themselves. Fly half Stephen Larkham, not the rebellious type, was guest at a corporate lunch on Thursday and was asked some very direct questions about what had gone wrong at the Gabba. He gave some very direct answers. 'I think that the style of game we went into the game with, of spinning the ball wide hoping to catch their defensive weakness out there,

Martin Johnson rises high at the line out. Following pages: Joe Roff crosses for his first try, beginning the Wallaby fightback.

didn't allow myself or the rest of the team to really get into the game,' said Larkham. 'My job was to get the ball wide and that doesn't really get our forwards into the game. It didn't get me into the game. It wasn't my natural game.'

The Wallabies had made three changes to their starting line-up. Prop Rod Moore came in for the injured Glenn Panoho, Michael Foley did likewise for the injured Jeremy Paul, while Matt Burke was to play full back instead of Chris Latham and also take over kicking duties.

The Wallabies faced their greatest test under Rod Macqueen. He had brought them four years of success, of rising to every challenge put before them. This was the toughest of the lot. He knew and their fans knew that the Lions had been the better team by a considerable distance in the first Test. Off the field, things had gone no better. The Lions fans had outnumbered, out-coloured and outsung the Wallaby supporters at the Gabba. The Australians did not want to see a repeat of that. Managing director John O'Neill reached into the ARU coffers and pledged $40,000 (£15,000) to kit out Wallaby fans with gold T-shirts and scarves.

It made for some backdrop. Melbourne's Colonial Stadium is a fine piece of architecture. While authorities in England faff about wondering what to do with Wembley, the real sporting progressives just get ahead and build new stadiums. The Colonial is only a couple of miles away from the all-consuming, oh-so-impressive 110,000-capacity Melbourne Cricket Ground. The Colonial holds 55,000, although a ground record of 56,605 actually managed to squeeze in.

The roof was closed, as it had been for the Mandela Cup game between South Africa and Australia the year before. The Lions had not raised any significant objections. 'We're not overly worried about it,' said Lenihan. 'I personally think rugby should be exposed to the elements, but I guess the scrum would prefer a drier sod.'

As it was, the scrum got their drier sod. It rained heavily throughout Saturday. The skies had cleared by evening time. Outside, Melbourne was buzzing.

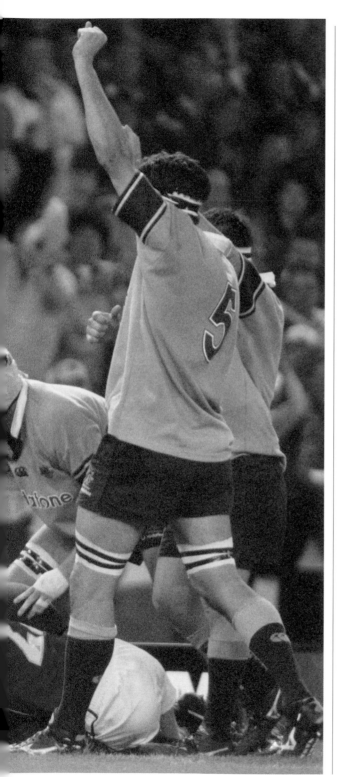

Matt Burke is somewhere in there, having scored Australia's third try. The full back ended the match with a haul of 25 points.

Tickets were changing hands for $750 (£300), sold on by what the Australians call 'scalpers', a far more suggestive term than our own word, tout.

The Australians revved up the atmosphere for all it was worth. A lot of it was very good – rock bands, proper fireworks not the damp squibs that they have on offer at Twickenham, dancing lads and lasses representing all the respective countries. But why do all these places employ a shrieking chimpanzee to look after the PA system? The crowd are more than capable of generating their own noise without some trumped-up halfwit barking at them to get involved. No matter. The place was jumping by the time kick-off came round. The Lions had made one late change, with Austin Healey forced to pull out with a bruised thigh to be replaced by Neil Jenkins.

The match lived up to its billing in the first half. There were several rollicking exchanges as both teams tested the other out. The Wallabies were far more on their mettle than the week before. For example, Owen Finegan on the flank was twice the player he had been at the Gabba. John Eales was also in better shape. The Wallabies attacked the Lions at the line out and the scrum. Much of what they did in the line out was illegal, with Martin Johnson being pulled down at the front to stop the Lions getting any momentum at the maul. It was one of the few areas in which the Wallabies did find favour with South African referee Jonathan Kaplan. He pinged them at the breakdown time and again.

There was evidence of nerves from both sides in the early stages. Matt Perry hoofed it out on the full, while Larkham was off-key on the other side. The Lions, though, had an assured look about them, picking up where they had left off the week before. In the fifth minute they almost did what they had done the week before – score a sensational try. Jonny Wilkinson put Dafydd James into a hole just inside the Lions ten-metre line. It was a beautiful piece of work – well orchestrated by Wilkinson and splendidly timed by James. If only the Welsh wing had been able to finish the sequence off. He ran with blinkers, missing the

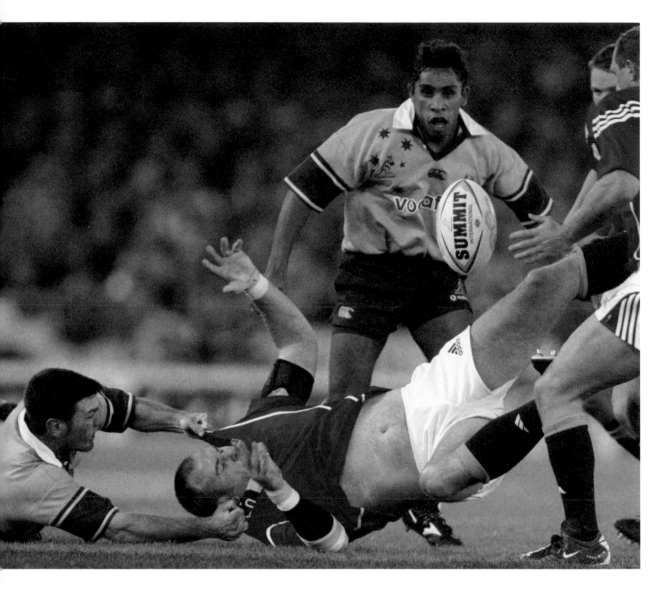

Lions No. 8 Scott Quinnell manages to offload as he is unceremoniously dumped by Wallaby centre Daniel Herbert.

men outside him and was held in the tackle just on the Wallaby 22. A try then – and there should have been a try then – and all the Wallaby self-doubts from the previous week might have surfaced.

There was no try. But the initiative remained firmly with the Lions throughout the rest of the half. Wilkinson knocked over a couple of early penalties before Burke got one back for Australia in the 20th minute. The Lions kept pressing. Brian O'Driscoll

was just lassoed from behind by George Smith after one typical break. In the 27th minute there was another piece of wizardry from the Irishman. He chipped and with a flying leap somehow managed to take a catch, from where the ball went back infield to Wilkinson. The fly half spotted a Lions shirt wide on the left and punted wide. Out here was Richard Hill who closed in on Andrew Walker as the Wallabies scrambled the ball into touch.

From the line out, the Lions, for once, managed to get their maul on the move and at the end of it was Neil Back. Wilkinson missed the conversion, and the score stood at 11-3. The Lions were pegged back by three points at the interval as Burke slotted another goal, an insufficient return for the Lions for their domination of both territory and possession.

Both Grewcock and Johnson had managed to gallop clear on a couple of occasions. Scott Quinnell was a massively influential figure, so too Richard Hill. The England flanker, though, was hit by a wild, high tackle from Nathan Grey in the 37th minute. He was led from the field clutching a bloody nose. He returned a few minutes later, but it was a futile gesture. He didn't reappear for the second half, Martin Corry taking up the cudgels. Hill had concussion and was out of the tour. Grey was to be cited by the Lions, but no action was taken. It was a disgraceful turn of events.

Despite all this there was no other sense at half-time but that we were in the middle of a fascinating Test match, one that once again seemed to be shaping up in the Lions' favour. Within seven minutes that theory had been well and truly exploded. Just 32 seconds after the restart, Jonny Wilkinson flung a rash pass down the narrow side in the direction of Rob Henderson and Dafydd James. Unfortunately it was also in the direction of Joe Roff. The Wallaby wing needed no second bidding, outstripping the Lions cover defence to get in – just – at the corner. Kaplan went to the video ref, but there was no doubting the score. It was to get worse. Eight minutes later a Lions scrum disintegrated some 30 metres out. In the melee, Eales latched on to the ball and headed goalwards. A quick flurry of Wallaby hands and there was Roff again heading for the corner, escaping the clutches of James and stepping inside Jason Robinson at the death. Burke, who had kicked a penalty goal a couple of minutes before, converted to make the score 21-11 with just eight minutes of the half gone.

It was a devastating turnaround in fortunes. And it completely did for the Lions. They wilted. The two sucker punches seemed to drain their morale and self-belief. They suddenly looked like a side that had been playing for 11 months and on the

---

Alarm bells ring all over Britain and Ireland as Jonny Wilkinson is stretchered off with what was thought might be a broken leg.

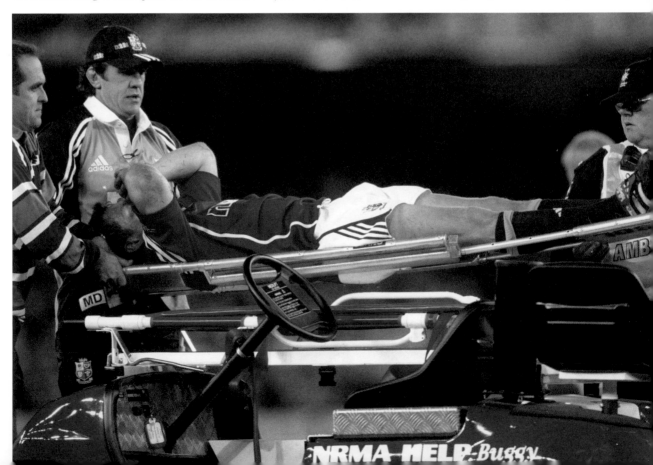

Australian prime minister John Howard congratulates the Wallabies after their series-levelling destruction of the Lions.

road for six weeks. Wilkinson got a penalty goal back, but the Wallabies were in the driving seat. It was no surprise when in the 65th minute, after a good spell of phase play, Burke was sent on his way to the try line by a shrewd pass from Finegan. Burke himself converted and was to kick three more goals to finish with 25 points in all.

There were more woes for the Lions. First Wilkinson was forced off with a nasty-looking leg injury, followed by Rob Howley clutching his ribs. The Lions were broken in body and spirit. The final score was 35-14, a record defeat for the Lions against the Wallabies. How had it come to this? 'We self-destructed,' was Martin Johnson's assessment. And so they had. 'If you give the Wallabies just one sniff they'll take it. We've got a very battered and bruised squad and we will have to rouse ourselves for one massive effort next week.'

Graham Henry pinpointed where it had all gone wrong. 'We didn't get the points we should have done in the first half,' said Henry. 'If we'd taken them it would have given us momentum. It was very difficult to catch up once they'd got their points on the board.'

Johnson and hooker Keith Wood knew instantly that this was the most significant moment on the entire tour. If heads dropped now, they would never come back up again. They both made impassioned speeches in the changing room afterwards. It was straightforward stuff but expressed forcibly and with great integrity. They had all come this far and there was little point stacking cards now. If the Lions shirt really did mean something, then they had to get behind it now, now when they were at their most tired and vulnerable. They all had to commit to the cause.

They did. And they headed north to Sydney with the series all square. It doesn't come much better or much bigger than this.

ARE PROUD TO SUPPORT

WOUNDED PRIDE

The Official Book of the Lions in Australia 2001

Match views: Second Test

Martin Johnson

You could tell from the demeanour of the Lions hierarchy the exact result, as if it were on a scoreboard behind them, as they dragged themselves reluctantly to explain themselves to the media. The sourness was evident early, when Martin Johnson described as 'stupid' a question regarding the technical defects of his pack and then proceeded to condemn his forwards' efforts:

'They shifted our scrum, got us on the back foot and kept us off balance. We were outplayed. We self-destructed and let ourselves down badly. We did not function as a unified eight. I hope it's mental rather than physical.'

Graham Henry

The Lions coach stated the obvious when he commented:

'We did not get enough points in that first half, when we had clear opportunities to build up a large lead. We turned ball over that we should have retained. When we fell behind we were chasing the game and became so desperate that we gave Burke those penalties that took the score even further away from us. But the turning point was undoubtedly Roff's interception try right at the start of the second half.'

Donal Lenihan and Richard Hill

There is usually a meaty row following modern Tests, and this time the dispute involved Australian centre Nathan Grey's tackle on Richard Hill, which removed the flanker from the series. Lions manager Donal Lenihan was fuming with indignation when no action was taken against Grey for concussing Hill with his elbow. The independent citing commissioner, David Gray from New Zealand, declined to take action, and a rumour swept the Lions camp that he considered a 'live' view of the incident sufficient and did not bother to watch the video because he had to catch a plane back to New Zealand:

'We are unhappy about the way Richard was injured,' raged Lenihan. *'We told the citing commissioner that we wanted to cite Grey, but he said that there was no*

No way through this time, but Wallaby full back Matt Burke scored a try plus 20 points with the boot to bring his side victory.

case for such a course. There is no right of appeal and we are surprised and disappointed about this outcome, which leaves Grey free to play in the deciding Test. By contrast we lost Colin Charvis for this Melbourne Test when he was cited and banned for a far less serious incident in Brisbane.'

Hill said: 'The tackle caused me memory loss and that is one symptom of concussion.'

Phil Larder

Larder, the Lions defence coach and the world's leading expert in the definition of legal and illegal tackles, said:
'The elbow to the jaw was foul play. In rugby league I would expect a player who perpetrated such a tackle to be suspended for six months, and I see no reason why rugby union should not have similarly rigorous standards of punishment. The elbow is a lethal weapon.'

Keith Wood

The Lions hooker summed up the determination not to let the situation deteriorate further:
'I would rather contemplate suicide than consider a series defeat. We certainly took our foot off the pedal and a win is impossible when you do that against Australia's all-encompassing game. We made silly mistakes and I have to confess that our scrum was disappointing.'

Rod Macqueen

Australia's coach took officials and players by surprise by announcing that he would stand down at the end of the series rather than after the Tri-Nations:
'Better to go sooner rather than later. You can be effective only for so long. Your enthusiasm can fade in a stressful job. Rugby has never been my entire life, and Australia will be in good hands with the new man, Eddie Jones.'

John Eales

Australia's captain commended his coach – 'He will remain one of the great figures of Wallaby rugby' – and explained the improvement between Tests one and two:
'We have always been our own harshest critics and acknowledged that we had to apply our known skills with a more competitive edge. Even when we were trailing in the first half I was convinced that if we could get some possession we would turn things around. Fortunately, the Lions gave us that vital bit of possession for Roff's score.'

Two-try hero Joe Roff salutes the crowd after Australia's record defeat of the Lions at the Colonial Stadium, Melbourne.

Reflections: Second Test

COMMENTS FROM THE LIONS COACH

Graham Henry in conversation with Ian Robertson

How differently do you think the Australians prepared in their attitude and approach to the second Test?

Hugely. They had a game under their belt and because of the psychological situation of losing the first Test, their preparation was ideal.

If you look at the first half you must have been very satisfied with the performance of the Lions but very worried that the chances weren't actually turned into points?

Exactly. We created a handful of scoring chances when we breached their defensive wall and there is no doubt that we should have scored a couple of tries. If we had led by a comfortable margin at half-time, there would have been a good chance the Australians wouldn't have had the confidence to launch their recovery in the second half.

What were the crucial areas that went wrong in not scoring those points?

Well, I don't think we had enough field position. We played a lot of rugby in our own half. We busted the line five times in the first half from a long distance out and we didn't complete those opportunities. There were some real opportunities, particularly when Dafydd James broke down the middle, and if he'd passed right instead of left we would have scored under the sticks. I think our biggest problem is we're not getting enough field positions in the game and so when we attack and break the line we've got a long distance to travel before we get over the try line. Our scrum wasn't as potent as in the first Test, our line out wasn't as smooth as in the first Test, and so there are lots of things we need to work on for the third Test in Sydney.

In the line out I've noticed you throw to the back quite a lot and it's gone wrong quite a lot. When you've thrown to the front and the middle you've won it. When you've thrown long it's not been

straight several times or thrown over the top. Are you persisting with the long ball because it's the best attacking weapon or is the line out a real cause for concern?

It's the best attacking weapon for the backs if you can get the ball off the back of the line out, but obviously it's more difficult to throw it there so we have had some problems. We also didn't have a specialist line-out player at the back end in the second Test, whereas we did have in the first Test. I mean we wanted to play Hill, we wanted to play Back and we wanted to play Quinnell, which meant we didn't have a real specialist line-out player. We tried to make Richard Hill into that and he did pretty well. It's just getting that balance right and sometimes it's not easy.

At half-time when you went in to see the team were you still in confident mood?

I think we felt like the players did. We had a lot of opportunities which we didn't take. We hoped that that wasn't going to affect the result of the game but eventually it did. I think there was some apprehension at half-time. We'd played a lot of rugby but didn't have the points to show for it. Perhaps we should have been up 20-6 at half-time instead of 11-6, and the fact that we were not, largely through our own fault, probably cost us the game.

And in the second half, we know there was an interception early on and that was five points, but how do you explain the complete change in the performance of both sides?

Well, I think the intercept try was a real body blow. It knocked our confidence to some extent and gave the Australians a real boost, and then some eight or nine minutes later when our scrum disintegrated and Roff scored again that just gave the Australians enough extra momentum to get back their confidence, and they went on to play some very good rugby. As far as we were concerned, we lost the momentum we had in the first half and suddenly the whole complexion of the match had changed. At the start of the second half we were leading 11-6, and ten minutes later we were trailing 21-11. We then were forced to try and play catch-up rugby for the rest of the game, and against the world champions that was never going to be easy.

You brought Iain Balshaw on. Was that to try and give you more options?

He's a good athlete Iain Balshaw, and at that stage we were quite a few points behind on the scoreboard and were looking for any option that would have given us a bit more athleticism in the back three. We had to play catch-up and we thought he might be a better catch-up player than Matt Perry.

How deflated were you immediately after the final whistle, and three days later do you feel not so bad about what happened? Are you now looking forward to the third Test?

I think the guys, the whole party, were pretty disappointed with the result of the second Test. It was a big opportunity for us. I think the Australians were struggling with their confidence, and it showed in the first half. We had an opportunity to

Iain Balshaw, on as replacement full back for Matt Perry, brings Stephen Larkham to a halt as the Lions play catch-up.

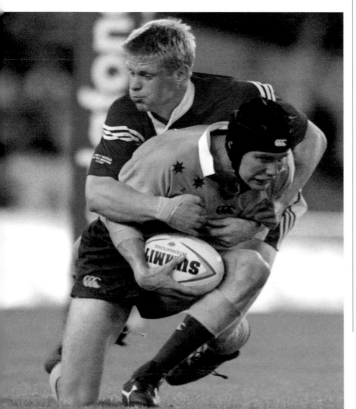

put the Test series away and it didn't happen, so that's disappointing. You just can't stay up there at your absolute peak for three weeks. It's impossible to stay on a high for three Tests in a row, and the guys slipped off their perch a few notches in the second half of the second Test. We had a very good week between the first and second Tests. The guys trained very well, the best they've trained on tour quite frankly. I think the confidence was pretty high. We struck an Australian side who weren't underdone like they were in the first Test and they were very sharp mentally. The guys have suffered a bit of a reaction after the defeat on Saturday. The mood of the party was a bit down on the Sunday and Monday, and I was a little concerned about it when we went training on Monday. We're a quiet camp really, but today [Tuesday] everyone was much more bubbly and they trained pretty well.

Looking ahead to the third Test, there's quite an air of optimism around now, and in fact you've got seven of the eight forwards who won the forward battle in the first Test and the first half of the second Test, and you've got five of the backs who dominated the first Test, so there's no reason why you shouldn't go out to win this third Test.

We're positive in the camp. I don't know how positive people are outside the camp. We think that if we can play to our full potential and we are not dogged by injuries then we can win the third Test.

It just needs the forwards to stay on top the whole 80 minutes.

That would be a huge plus. We just need to play better. We dominated the scrums in the first Test, we were reversed in the second and we've got to reverse that again. We've got to get more fluency in the line out. Our ball at the tackle area needs to be more fluid. We're under pressure there to maintain it and we need to play in their end of the paddock. We've got the ability to break the line, as everybody can see, and we can break down the Australian defence, we're just having trouble completing those movements from a long distance out. We need to play the game in their half of the field and not have to launch our attacks from 50 or 60 metres out. Our defence is very good. So we're hopeful.

FROM AN AUSTRALIAN VIEWPOINT
by MICHAEL LYNAGH

I have never seen such dramatically different halves of rugby in one match. It was almost like the two teams agreed before the match to take turns with the ball. I can imagine John Eales and Martin Johnson talking before the match: 'You have the ball in the first half, and we'll have it in the second'.

At half-time the Wallabies were not in the game. The Lions were dictating every aspect as they had done for most of the match a week earlier in Brisbane. The only positive that Eales's team could take out of the first half was that they were only five points adrift. The Wallabies needed to be gifted something by the Lions.

It came in the first minute of the second half. Jonny Wilkinson spotted a three on two overlap down the short right-hand side. The decision to run the ball was correct, the execution wasn't. Instead of using the next man, Wilkinson tried to cut him out to give the man after him the run. Joe Roff spotted the danger, and stepping in from his wing, took the ball, sprinted to the corner to score and brought Australia back into the contest.

Many have said that this pass changed the whole Test match. Without doubt this is true, but for me the defining moment in the game came a short time after. The Lions had a centre-field scrum in Australian territory. In Brisbane they had scored from a very similar position by bringing O'Driscoll and Robinson to run together down the right. It worked a charm and James scored in the corner.

As the scrum went down in Melbourne, I could see the same three Lions looming into position on the right of the scrummage. The Wallaby scrum, which has always been marked down as a potential weakness, picked this moment to change the direction of events. They screwed the Lions scrum and then powered over the top of it. The Lions forwards were all over the place. Eales swooped on the ball, Smith cleaned out, then Gregan and Larkham combined to put Roff on a 40-metre sprint into the same corner.

The momentum had swung to the Wallabies, and they certainly knew what to do with it. They piled on the pressure, and all of a sudden the Lions

defence were waiting for the runners to come to them. The big ball carriers, Kefu and Finegan, were starting to make ground, giving Gregan the room to pick up his runners coming from lovely angles that kept the Lions defence guessing.

It is an interesting fact that in the two Tests to date the Wallabies have finished on top of their opponents. Along with this the Lions have picked up an incredible number of injuries on this tour. I think that the reason for these two problems is the same thing. Is the long season starting to take its toll? The Wallabies are only halfway through their season, and although they have been a bit rusty due to the lack of matches, they appear to be the fresher of the two teams as the games wear on. I am not saying the Lions are unfit – far from it. What I am suggesting is that the number of games some of the players have played this year, combined with the arduous tour itinerary and training, is starting to show.

If this is the case, at least the Lions have a week to recover and regroup at the Sydney beachside suburb of Manly. They will need to be fresh and on song next Saturday night, as the momentum the Wallabies gained in Melbourne will not be lost in transit when they run out onto the pitch this weekend at Stadium Australia.

My ball! Skipper John Eales rampages through the Lions forwards as the Wallabies impose themselves at Melbourne.

First National
is pleased
to support
WOUNDED PRIDE
The Official Book of the Lions in Australia 2001

Providing point of sale finance through:

- Home Improvement Loans
- Holiday Ownership Loans
- First Mortgages
- Secured Personal Loans

For more information please visit our website
www.firstnat.co.uk

6. The Third Test

Everything had changed – the mood, the personnel; even the damn weather had taken a turn for the worse. The Lions squad checked back into the Park Royal Pacific on Manly seafront for the second time on this trip. Three weeks earlier they had been gearing towards the first Test. The skies were clear and there was a decent degree of optimism in the air.

Now, as they filed off the bus from the airport in the early evening, their thoughts were darker. So too was the ocean behind them. Record five-metre winter swells had been recorded as the east coast was battered by the remnants of the typhoon that

Forget Melbourne, this is Sydney. Lions fans gather on the steps of the Opera House ahead of the third and deciding Test.

had lashed Asia a few days earlier. If the surfers were happy at developments that weekend, the Lions were not.

They realised that they had blown a gilt-edged chance to wrap up the series in Melbourne. Everything had been in their favour. They were riding a wave of buoyant good feeling from the Gabba Test, a sense of self-belief that had manifested itself so tellingly during the first half in Melbourne. Victoria's capital city had also been packed with British and Irish fans. It was the crossover point in the series and the Test was the time of optimum support. The Aussies would be fighting back in Sydney, reclaiming their turf.

And then it had all turned in eight daft minutes. The Lions had gifted the Wallabies two tries and with them the match. Had the series also gone down the tubes? That was the gloomy thought – unstated in many minds, for that way defeatism lies – that hung in the Sydney air.

There were other reasons for the downbeat mood. Two more players, Rob Howley and Richard Hill, were out of contention. Howley had left the field clutching his ribs a few minutes before the final whistle. By midnight it was confirmed that a couple of them were cracked. Hill had been led off just before half-time with blood streaming from his nose after a vicious tackle from Wallaby centre Nathan Grey. The England flanker made a valiant attempt to get back on the field but bowed to the inevitable at the break. 'My memory was a bit confused,' said Hill. 'I don't remember much about the incident itself. Johnno had fired a pass my way but it had bounced off my body. I was hit from the side, got a bang on the jaw and that was it.'

Hill may not have remembered much about it. The Lions management did. They felt that Grey had launched a high and violent tackle on Hill and ought to have faced disciplinary action for it. The independent match commissioner, New Zealander David Gray, thought differently.

The Lions bridled and fumed but there was to be no recourse to disciplinary action. The Aussies themselves were listening and wondered just who the pot was to call the kettle black. Their fly half Stephen Larkham had been hammered late at least twice, once by Rob Henderson and once by Scott Quinnell. Both tackles, marginally late, had been picked up and dealt with by referee Jonathan Kaplan. Even so, the Australians, never ones to miss a chance to retaliate, sent the ball whining back over the net. This time it was left to former Wallaby captain Simon Poidevin to send the service crashing down. 'Too many times during the second Test Stephen Larkham was unfairly targeted and it was obvious that the Lions were trying to wipe him out,' said Poidevin.

True. Any side with any sense would want to put Larkham out of the game. The issue of legality is the only point of concern. 'You've got to put guys like Larkham under pressure,' said Phil Larder. 'You need to close his space down because he's the bloke that calls the shots. The more he's on the floor the better. If he's on his backside then he's out of the game.'

And so the stakes were raised once again, with verbal thrust and counter-thrust. Rugby in Australia has to scrap for every column inch of newspaper space with rugby league and Australian Rules football, and it was committing all its resources to doing just that. Not a day was to pass on the entire trip when some angle or other was not tweaked for all it was worth. The Lions were not averse to their own media manipulation either, through blunt denial or smokescreens or concealment of truths. It was not always easy to distinguish between truth and half-truth.

That is why the news on Jonny Wilkinson was initially treated with scepticism. From the moment that the England fly half was taken from the field in considerable distress, it looked for all the world as if his tour was over. And yet the initial prognosis

was that there might yet be some hope for Wilkinson. There was no obvious fracture visible, just severe bruising of the lower left leg. Wilkinson had stayed behind in Melbourne with Howley and Hill, unable to fly because of the increased pressure that the flight would put upon the bruising. He was put in plaster as a precaution.

Administering the tender loving care as he had on two previous Lions tours was Dr James Robson. A Cumbrian by birth, a GP and physiotherapist by

Rob Howley being attended by James Robson during the second Test. Howley was one of a staggering number of tour casualties.

trade, and an all-round good bloke by inclination, Robson had burnt the candle at every end on this trip. The toll of injuries and ailments had taxed even a man of his immense resources. 'I've had 29 nights here,' he said on Tuesday evening. 'And I've been woken up after going to bed on 22 of them. I've never known this level of work. I wouldn't swop it for anything, of course, and I'd rather people did come to me when they need medical advice rather than wait for the morning, but it has been exceptionally busy. I got a bit depressed by it all one evening so went out with some Australian friends, who treated me to a fabulous, very expensive bottle of red wine, Penfolds Hermitage. It was a great evening and I was without my mobile phone for the first time on tour. I felt good, only to get back and see this queue outside my door.

Something has to be done about all this. Some of the injuries are due just to ill luck. But the demands on players are another reason. The sheer physicality of the game is now 40 per cent or so higher than it was when I was first with the Lions in 1993 in New Zealand. And the length of the season is just ridiculous. The career span of players will get shorter and shorter. Something has to be done about it.'

Strong, heartfelt words. We all know what will be done about it – absolutely nothing. Only a few days earlier many of us had listened in disbelief as the International Board announced that it was looking to stage an annual northern hemisphere against southern hemisphere fixture. 'It's only one more match and will be a great opportunity to showcase rugby,' said IB chairman Vernon Pugh.

One more match – and with those words the IB came tumbling down from the moral high ground. The players are being flogged from pillar to post.

A sight to cheer Lions hearts. Injury scare Jonny Wilkinson, here with Brian O'Driscoll, is up and running in time for the third Test.

Keith Wood, personification of the Lions spirit. 'Do you think that we are going to lie down at this stage?'

No one is prepared to give way. No one is prepared to step off the money-grasping treadmill and cede any ground. Each chases the other. The game wants more money to fund professionalism and development, while the players want more money to compensate them for the horrendous workload. The IB will get its players for its showcase game because it will buy them off. That's the currency the sport trades in and it is being devalued by the year.

Robson had good news on Wilkinson that Tuesday evening. 'He will be fit to play,' said Robson. 'He's at 70-30 and I would expect him to maintain that rate of improvement.' Robson is not a man for doublespeak, for playing the media game to suit whatever end. If he said that Wilkinson would be fit to play, then Wilkinson would be fit to play. The news gave the camp a huge fillip. The low of Saturday and Sunday night had now bottomed out. The barometer was swinging back

towards high pressure. A tour, and a Lions tour in particular, has so many mood shifts. It's so important for players, and management, not to panic, not to get alarmed by a seeming decline and act in haste. There had been times on the trip when the players had been put through too much as the management piled in to ensure that all the working parts were in good order come the Test series.

At this stage there was no need to rev up the troops. All the revving that could be done had been done. It was imperative that the players took a lead role in the week's preparation, for they alone knew what state their bodies and souls were in. They knew what it would take for the one last push. Keith Wood had been a key figure on the 1997 tour. He was assuming the same mantle again. 'Do you think that we are going to lie down at this stage and not get our heads around winning?' said Wood. 'Of course not. Just because we lost the match in Melbourne does not mean that we have lost the series. Far from it. We're on an even keel. This is a fabulously exciting thing, to be going into the decider on a Lions tour. It's a scary proposition but one that you absolutely have to relish. The thought of it overrides everything – fatigue, bruises, bumps and all those sort of things. The guys may be sore all right but the desire is there.'

second best) suggested that here was a squad that was set on making the most of its last week as Lions. They were gathering themselves for one last blast. The Monday afternoon splash in the Pacific was a moment of light relief. There had not been many on tour. There would not be many ahead.

The Lions named their team, as scheduled, on Wednesday lunchtime. The Wallabies delayed their announcement until Thursday. They had doubts over Larkham and second-row David Giffin. The

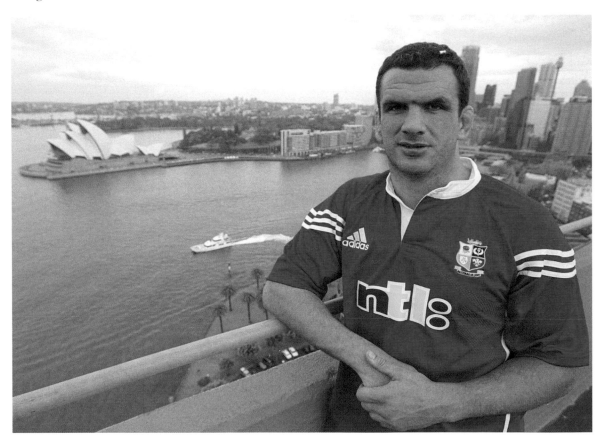

Martin Johnson does the Harbour Bridge Climb, a must-do for any Sydney visitor. Would he be on top of the world come Saturday?

You could sense a shift in the breeze. The Wilkinson news had had a galvanising effect. Now, a few blokes frolicking in the Manly waves is not necessarily the most reliable portent for a rugby match, but the sight of Johnson, Wood, Healey and Morris fighting the surf (and coming off a distinct

Lions seemingly had no more real injury concerns, although several players, such as centres Brian O'Driscoll and Rob Henderson and No. 8 Scott Quinnell, were carrying knocks. All three players were in the line-up for the decisive Test at Stadium Australia on Saturday evening.

So too were the tour 'Bad Boys', Matt Dawson and Austin Healey. Healey was to take the place of Dafydd James, the Welshman paying the price for the fluffed chance in the second Test. The other change saw Martin Corry come into the back row.

Healey had been chosen for the tour as a scrum half. Now here he was as the Lions trump card against the Wallabies. 'We think that he will give us another dimension,' said Graham Henry.

It would have been nice to know what Healey thought. Or Dawson. Or Wilkinson. All three players were exciting interest for various reasons. All three were pulled from the media press conference that Wednesday afternoon. Only a handful of players were made available. It was another example of the Lions management not tuning in to the role of the media. It was as if they held them personally responsible for the glitches that had occurred rather than seeing them as a means of keeping their vast band of followers, both at home and in Australia, fully informed of what was going on. In a professional era there are obligations to be met. On the media front those obligations were not always fully met.

Healey in fact did speak, a couple of journalists nabbing him as he walked through the hotel. His views were important for the simple reason that he had been glaringly upstaged by his opposite number, Joe Roff, when England played Australia back in November, the Wallaby wing twice cutting up Healey. Here was the rematch. 'There will be people expecting him to do the same thing,' said Healey. 'I'll just do my best to eradicate all that sort of thing. It's not just a one-on-one battle out there. I've got a roving brief. That's the only way I know how to play. I'm not the world's best defender or ball carrier or even finisher, but I know that I will do all the other stuff to the best of my ability. This has been a tour of ups and downs. You can take all the downs as long as you finish on a high.'

Little did he know what lay in store for him. Dawson's selection was inevitable once Howley had been forced to pull out. The management had stated that Dawsongate was a closed matter and had been dealt with internally at the time. In rugby terms, they were as good as their word. 'I've worked hard on this trip in order to be ready when the opportunity came my way,' said Dawson. 'It's come my way and it's up to me to show what I can do. That doesn't mean that I should force things.

No, the main thing is to get the best out of all those around me. And, then, if the chance comes to break, I break. The middle part of the tour was a difficult time because of all the pressure I brought on myself. But we've all moved on. And now we have the biggest match that most of us have ever played in.'

The forwards had put in a lot of work on their scrummaging, smarting after their difficulties the week before. 'I'm not sure that we needed a kick up the arse,' said tight-head Phil Vickery. 'But we certainly got one. It was frustrating and something we've had to put to rights.'

The squad paid a visit to Stadium Australia on Thursday, almost an hour's run by bus from their Manly base. They would have to spend an unusually long time travelling on Saturday afternoon and needed to acclimatise. The stadium, in the process of being reconfigured from its Olympic shape and size, down from 110,000 to 85,000, is not actually the most breathtaking in the world: impressive, yes, but open and rather bare. The memories rather than the monument are what enthral. The feel-good factor of the Sydney Games was still bubbling away and several players got a kick out of tracing the same steps that the likes of Cathy Freeman had taken nine months earlier.

Across town, the Wallabies were coming clean on their own injury problems. Larkham and Giffin were both out, to be replaced by Elton Flatley, an experienced back-up, and Brumbies lock Justin Harrison, who was not. The uncapped Harrison, 27, did not play rugby at all until the age of 19. He took up with a bunch of rugby blokes at Lismore University. '"Just stand four back in the line out and catch the ball when we throw it to you" was the only advice they gave me,' said Harrison.

Good advice too. Harrison had been doing a lot of catching ever since. He had been the outstanding performer in that year's Super-12. He had done a similar number for Australia A in the Lions' only midweek defeat and then led the charge in the Brumbies game against the Lions. That game had brought him into spiky confrontation with Healey. The pair had had a running spat throughout the game. Healey had seemingly had the last word when he touched down for the try

The world champion Wallabies in training at Randwick Army Barracks. Could Saturday herald the Twilight of the Gods?

that brought the scores level, teeing up Matt Dawson's dramatic match-winning conversion.

Our Austin, however, wasn't quite finished yet. There were more words to come. Harsh, spiteful, all appearing under his byline in *The Guardian* and quoted back all across the Australian newspapers on the morning of the third Test. By that time, calamity had befallen Healey himself, the wing having to pull out with a bulging disc. He had first felt a sharp pain on Thursday. On Friday he had to sit out the final run-through at Manly Oval. On Saturday morning at first light he had an MRI scan. It confirmed what he already knew – that he did not have a cat in hell's chance of taking the field.

Justin Harrison might have relished the chance of a few words with Healey that afternoon. Healey had launched an astonishing attack on the Brumbies lock, calling him variously 'a plod', 'a plank' and 'an ape'. Healey had also had a go at the Australian male, the media and the country itself. Apart from that, he loved the place. Under the heading 'And for our finale… Stuffing the arrogant Aussies', Healey said: 'Anything we say on this tour comes back down this way with a whole lot of spin. Well, spin this, you Aussies: Up Yours. Is that enough to get into the Sydney Morning Sun Telegraph Herald Load of Shite? If ever I wanted to do anything it was beat you lot.'

On and on went Healey. The Australians would have lapped it up. 'It was a ready-made team talk for Rod Macqueen,' as Henry was to put it later. The Lions coach had only learnt of the piece when chatting to a couple of journalists in the hotel lobby on Saturday morning. He was not best pleased. 'I find it astonishing that a player can give the opposition the ammunition with which to prepare for a game,' said Henry.

Henry gave enough hints, too, that Healey might well have found himself bumped out of the Test side if that had been an option. As it was, Healey was pumped full of valium (the coach might have needed a couple of shots after reading the papers) to counter the pain, and Henry was busy scratching around for a back-up scrum half. Dafydd James was to fill in for Healey, but there was now no cover for Dawson.

Quite how the management let events come to this pass is a puzzle. They had been asked on Sunday what the contingency plan was and had replied that as there was no midweek game then there was no need to send for anyone else to back up Dawson and Healey. Oh yes there was. And by Friday night the management's only options lay in either throwing in Neil Back at the deep end were Dawson to be forced off or heading out into the streets to summon an emergency replacement from the ranks of players currently in Sydney on holiday.

Scotland scrum half Andy Nicol got the call on Friday night to report to the team hotel at 10 a.m. the next day. Nicol was leading a tour group and would certainly have had a few tales to tell after his 80 minutes on the Lions bench that evening. It was a daft state of affairs and a poor reflection on a management that had prided itself on getting the detail right.

There were one or two other details to attend to. Will Greenwood's ankle ligaments had suffered a reaction in training and he was forced to withdraw on Friday afternoon. Mark Taylor was called up, only to be bumped when Nicol was brought in. Iain Balshaw also had a touch of flu and was being dosed up.

The Wallabies were in much better order and looking to give their coach, Rod Macqueen, an emotional send-off. Macqueen was to stand down after the match, passing over the reins to Eddie Jones. In his three and a half years in charge, the Wallabies had swept the board, winning the World Cup, the Tri-Nations and the Bledisloe Cup. The Lions were Macqueen's final target.

The scene was set. There was a buzz about the bustling city of Sydney throughout Saturday. A few of us looked down from high up on the city's famous Harbour Bridge that morning and

wondered which of the teams would be reaching similar dizzy heights that evening.

It was some backdrop. The ARU had used every trick in the book to try and counter the massive presence of the red-clad Barmy Army. They had installed coloured sacks over the bucket seats at the end of the ground currently under reconstruction in order to provide a band of gold all round the lower seating area. Surprise, surprise, the vast contingent of Lions fans found themselves up in the gods at either end of the stadium. They would have to strain every larynx to make themselves heard. They strained every larynx.

The first half lived up to all expectations. It was fierce and it was relentless. There were mistakes made on both sides but no one could fail but to be rapt by the brutal intensity of the rugby. The Lions scrum was far more on its mettle than the week before and several times managed to get a little nudge on the Wallabies. In fact in the 20th minute they got a very big nudge on, marching the

Emergency call-up Andy Nicol watches the third Test unfold from the bench. In the end, his services were not required.

Wallabies back from a close-range scrum. For some inexplicable reason (other than the fact that his countrymen seem to have abandoned any notion of physically contesting the ball) New Zealand referee Paddy O'Brien called a halt and ordered the scrum to be reset. It was a daft decision and might well have cost the Lions dear in terms of momentum if they had not been able to touch down just a minute later. Three more scrums were re-formed as the Wallabies defended their line.

Smith, who sent Jason Robinson diving in at the corner for his tenth try of the tour. Wilkinson's conversion edged the Lions in front 10-9. The Lions fly half had earlier kicked a goal; Matt Burke had landed three penalties for the Wallabies.

As Wilkinson teed up his conversion attempt, there was the alarming sight on the near touch line of Dawson applying ice to his hamstring. He had been given a fearful shellacking at an early ruck (can't imagine why he of all people had been

Jason Robinson beats George Gregan to the corner to open the Lions try account at Stadium Australia.

From the fourth scrum, the Lions picked and drove. They were checked but went again. Henderson then hammered forward but was pulled down. The Lions forwards piled in to recycle. Dawson followed up, flashed the ball away to his left where Keith Wood was lurking. He fed Tom

targeted for such treatment) and his hamstring was now throbbing. Somehow, he stayed the distance.

There was thrust and counter-thrust. Both open-sides, Neil Back and George Smith, were having a terrific tussle to see who could filch most ball in the tackle. In the line out, too many Lions throws were missing their man and too much was being fired to the back. As half-time approached, it was clear that aspect of the Lions game needed attention.

The two kickers, Burke and Wilkinson, were not at their precise best, Wilkinson especially. His second miss of the evening came in the 38th minute, not a straightforward shot but one that he would expect to land, and had been landing, for England. Three points is not just important on the scoreboard. It also gives a side a boost at crucial times, usually being the reward for pressure exerted. Wilkinson had brought home the goodies on so many occasions. Yet he had not been at his deadly finest throughout the series. His strike rate, normally up around 80 per cent, was down in the mid-50s. Burke had had a better time of it in the second Test and was to come through strongly here. However, he made a pig's ear of one shot in the 40th minute, missing from around 25 metres.

Wallaby fans did not have to suffer too long. From the restart Harrison leapt to gather. The Wallaby pack pressed ahead. Owen Finegan punched forward, then came Toutai Kefu. Phase play – the Holy Grail of Wallaby rugby. They'd found it. The Lions defence was stretched. A final flurry of hands down the blind side, wing Joe Roff coming across to play link man and pass infield to Daniel Herbert for a try. It was a slick piece of play, Burke converting to put the Wallabies six points clear.

The Lions were far from done yet. They too were looking to build play and managed it right on the stroke of half-time. Rob Henderson did the initial damage with a trademark thrust through the middle. He was checked but the damage was done – the Wallaby defence was breached. The Lions threw everything at the Australian line. Back, Robinson, Wood, O'Driscoll, Johnson, Wilkinson – they all did their damnedest to make it happen. Thirteen phases of play in all could not yield the elusive second try. The Lions had to make do with a Wilkinson penalty to narrow the scoreline to 16-13 at the interval.

It had been an absorbing half's play, the most equal of the five halves contested so far in the Test series. Neither side had managed to slip the leash and get away. The forward battle was an equal contest, although the Lions did need to tighten up their line out. Behind the scrum, the various match winners, Roff and Walker, Robinson and O'Driscoll, were itching to get involved.

Matt Burke converts another shot at goal. In the duel of the kickers, he had the better of Jonny Wilkinson over the series.

There are many theories in sport, all peddled with great conviction at any stage of a contest: before, during and after. At this stage of a rugby match, the received wisdom is that the side that comes out of the traps well in the second half, the one that gets the all-important first try, will be the one that wins the day.

The Lions got an early try and they lost. Like all theories, sports theories bear only a passing semblance to reality. Sport always suckers us with unexpected twists. If it didn't we wouldn't keep coming back for more. The Lions, who had brought on Colin Charvis for the injured Scott Quinnell,

Daniel Herbert dives for the line to score the first of his two tries. Following pages: Jonny Wilkinson is in for the second Lions try.

began so forcefully. Just three minutes into the second half, Corry won a line out. The ball was pushed infield. Vickery made ground, as did Grewcock and Robinson. Wood made a big charge, followed by Henderson. The Wallabies were back-pedalling. Finally the ball went right to Wilkinson. One little trademark shuffle to leave Kefu in two minds and he was through. Wilkinson converted his own try to put the Lions four points clear at 20-16.

The advantage didn't last long. Within seven minutes Herbert had scored his second try. It all stemmed from a moment of pure panic from Charvis. The Wallabies had kicked deep into the Lions 22, where Charvis was covering. It was a Lions throw. For reasons known only to himself, Charvis took a quick throw to himself. Not quick enough, for he was immediately closed down. He then compounded his error by trying to blast away a left-footed clearance which only bounced along the ground into Wallaby hands. They drove hard and worked a field position. The Lions cleared their lines again but were still within their 22. The Wallabies won their line out, Nathan Grey clattered forward, then Kefu. A movement left, Foley linked with Herbert who was in at the corner. Burke converted. The pendulum swung again.

It went back the other way two minutes later when Herbert was sin-binned for a high tackle on Brian O'Driscoll. The Lions were not able to press home their advantage. Wilkinson kicked the goal for the offence to tie the scores at 23-23 and that was it. Game, set and match. For the third Test in succession the Lions failed to score a single point in the last quarter. What does this mean? They were unfit, unlucky or unable to raise their game when it mattered? A combination of all three.

There was a distinct impression that the Lions were playing at the limit of their capabilities, mental as much as physical. When the winds were with them, they were fine, but when they hit choppy waters they were not able to summon extra reserves of energy or initiative to get them out of trouble. These are fine margins we are talking about, but they are the margins that count.

They had a couple of chances, half-openings that great sides are able to capitalise on. With four minutes remaining, and the Lions trailing 29-23 from two further Burke penalties, they themselves were awarded a penalty. They opted to go for touch. Fair enough. They were well within the Wallaby 22. Now they had to make it count.

Defending teams in this position will invariably choose not to contest the line out. If they do and lose it, then they are vulnerable to the line-out drive, the very reason that the attacking team has set up position there in the first place. The Lions called for front ball, their banker option, to Martin Johnson. Standing opposite was Justin Harrison, a novice by comparison. Wallaby captain John Eales called a defensive ploy. Harrison objected. He felt he could get in front of Johnson. It was a big call. And it was the right one. Harrison plucked the ball from under Johnson's nose and the position was saved. 'I took a punt and it came off,' said Harrison. 'I didn't want to be a passenger in my first Test. I wanted to contribute, to do something special.'

He did that all right. The Lions had one final fling of the dice, Wilkinson finding clear water along the blind side in the very last sequence. The Lions had an overlap, a three on two. The final pass to Balshaw, however, did not go properly to hand and the Wallabies scrambled the ball away.

It was all over. As ever at the end of any monumental sporting contest, there was an air of unreality at the final whistle as the truth sinks in for both sides. The winners are able to cope with this – delirium is not the worst feeling in the world. For the losers, there is a crushing sense of gloom and anticlimax. All that effort and for what? It was little consolation for the players to be told that they had been part of a titanic series, that their feats had gripped people far and wide. If anything, that compounds the misery. The forlorn faces as the Lions players trudged down the tunnel told their own tale. First Matt Perry, then Rob Henderson, all utterly crestfallen.

They re-emerged to acknowledge their fans and then stood to watch the presentation ceremony. The Tom Richards Cup might so easily have been theirs. Their big chance had been in Melbourne, but they had allowed themselves to get rattled.

Daniel Herbert is in the right place at the right time again and crosses for Wallabies' second try.

And now, how would they be judged? As losers is the stark reality. Valiant or otherwise is neither here nor there. Lions tours are remembered solely for the achievements in the Test series. The 1997 Lions have been feted for four years as a hard-core unit that put it over the world champions of the time, the Springboks. Rarely mentioned is the fact that the Lions were on the back foot in both Tests, that if the Boks had had a goal-kicker of even middling note they would have won. Who cares? The history books show that the Lions triumphed 2-1 and that's all that matters.

The great high of the Gabba, the initial promise of Melbourne will quickly fade. There will be talk of opportunity missed – and there was – but it cannot erase the reality of the series scoreline. 'We came up short,' said Martin Johnson, never one to

gloat in victory and never one to duck the issue in defeat. 'From when the first whistle blows to when the last whistle sounds it's the players' game. It's our fault. It's as simple as that.'

Not quite. The Lions management will have to look within as well, analyse what went wrong and what went right. Quite whether Matt Dawson should have broken ranks with his mid-tour tales of internal dissent is an issue in itself. Leave that to one side. What has to be taken on board is that Dawson was not out of step with the feelings of several others. A happy camp is usually a productive one. For a side that spent so much time rehearsing set-piece, it was ironic that it should be the line out that let them down in the final Test.

Of course there were mitigating factors, not least the fact that the Lions were out on their feet. They never had more than 11 fit front-line players at training that final week. Almost the entire back line was shot to pieces. 'I've never been in that situation in 30 years of coaching,' said Henry. 'If you'd have known what we were going in with then you would not have given us a dog's chance.'

There were a few matters to attend to that Sunday morning as the 2001 Lions went their separate ways. The Healey row rumbled on. 'There is the possibility that he will be fined,' said Henry of the man who had already checked out of the hotel and was on his way to Hawaii on holiday.

Henry also suggested that he would recommend that players not be allowed to write columns on

World Cup, Tri-Nations, Bledisloe Cup and now the Lions. Eales, Stiles, Cockbain and Flatley celebrate being on top of the world.

Too much to bear. Henderson and Wilkinson are consoled by their fellow tourists after giving everything for the Lions.

future Lions tours. That's too sweeping and too trite a suggestion when you bear in mind that an in-house fly-on-the-wall documentary was being shot throughout this trip and that the coach himself was compiling a post-tour book. By all means close ranks, but the exclusion zone has to be total.

It had been a successful tour in some regards. The level of support and interest will ensure the commercial well-being of future Lions trips. Quite what format they take is a matter to be thrashed

out. Henry advocates shorter tours with the firm emphasis on Test matches. That will be a big break with tradition. Certainly the midweek side here were shunted into the sidings at an early stage.

There was some great rugby played across the six weeks. Several players – Brian O'Driscoll, Jason Robinson, Richard Hill – blossomed. A couple – Iain Balshaw, Scott Murray – knew that their reputations were in need of varnishing over the course of the next season.

The tour took on a different shape and hue almost by the day. Lee Smith had been right. Australia had been the place to be.

Born in Britain...

...loved the world over

As the official vehicle supplier to the 2001 Lions, Land Rover has much in common with these

very special sportsmen. Like guts, stamina and that real sense of purpose every adventurer requires.

Which is why it's so appropriate that the Lions will be taking the best 4x4 by far to Australia with

them. But why stop there? Call 0800 110 110 for an information pack - and let Discovery

take you further...

LIONS

official vehicle supplier

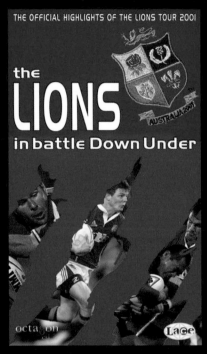

Match views: Third Test

Martin Johnson

It's a harsh, often unpalatable fact that participants have to win sporting contests. Coaches don't kick goals. Lions coach Graham Henry had his tour critics, internal and external. But he and his fellow coaches had prepared a squad that stood 23-23 with the final Test there to be won. Fortunately for the decreasing dignity of the tour, captain Martin Johnson acknowledged who was to blame:
'It was the players' fault. I told the team that this should be our 80 minutes. We came up short and it hurts.'

For the second successive Test Johnson, always proud of his line-out work, was compelled to concede that much of the trouble started in his area:
'Our discipline was poor, and conceding penalties and losing ball in the line out cost us promising positions. Australia were cute in the line out, and that was the difference between the sides, with their flanker George Smith being a step ahead of us.' But he had to point out: *'Half the players were held together by sticking tape. The tank was dry, but I could not have asked for more from my colleagues.'*

Justin Harrison

By a grimly predictable irony, new Wallaby lock Justin Harrison was man of the match, having been abused by injured Lion Austin Healey as 'a plank', 'a plod' and 'an ape'. Harrison's response came on the field and after, when he remarked:
'Not much command of the English language by Austin. I'm happy about the game I played and he can think about the game he only talked on his long flight home.'

Graham Henry

Naturally, former Wallabies climbed ferociously into Healey, and Lions coach Graham Henry was appalled that Healey should betray the tour:
'We would not have let his comments go if we had known. You are always going to get players who grizzle. I am amazed that a Lion should give the opposition a built-in team talk. I know the Australian animal and that was the ammunition Rod Macqueen would have needed. There are some things you think but don't say because they destroy the fabric of the team.'

Healey was also picked out by Henry on a separate issue, for his dedication to rugby:
'He played 53 games during the long season. They all play a ridiculous amount and that's the reason we could not train the Test team in the week before Sydney... It was a miracle that we ran Australia so

---

Names will never hurt me. Debutant and man of the match Justin Harrison holds aloft the series trophy, the Tom Richards Cup.

close. *Five or six potential Test guys did not play and up to a dozen will need prolonged treatment, possibly operations, when they get home. We did everything we could to win the series, but the bottom line is that we lost.'*

The Lions coach also agreed with skipper Johnson over problems in the line out:
'The line out was not as efficient as we expected.'

Martin Corry

One of the tour replacements and finally a battler in the Test team, Corry said:
'We should have won after playing Australia to a standstill in the middle of the match. That's what makes defeat feel so bitter.'

'What a bloody good way to go.' Rod Macqueen shares the last of his many momentous victories as Wallaby coach.

Matt Dawson

The Lions scrum half pointed out:
'We could manage only the penalty for Daniel Herbert's offence while he was off the pitch for ten minutes, and throughout our skill levels were hit-and-miss. Even so, we lost only to a late couple of penalties.'

Keith Wood

An emotional Lions hooker said:
'I was even beyond tears in a lonely, desolate dressing room.'

Rod Macqueen

Departing as coach of overwhelmingly the best team in the world, Macqueen stated:
'What a bloody good way to go. I bow out a happy man, having seen Australia so resilient under extreme conditions.'

Reflections: Third Test

Looking back at the third Test, it was a frustrating day at the office, wasn't it?

The build-up was actually far more frustrating than the match itself. We had so many injured players that we probably only had about two-thirds of the side on the training pitch at any one time and not even the same ten players. When you consider it was impossible and impractical to undertake any full sessions in preparation, what they did in that Test was really quite remarkable. We just patched the side up, got them on the field, and they gave 100 per cent – more than 100 per cent probably. It was a frustrating week.

Martin Johnson said afterwards that they were held together by sticky tape and bandages. Is that an accurate comment?

We certainly had an incredible number of injured players, and if the Test had been on the Wednesday, half of the eventual team would have been unavailable. It speaks volumes for the squad that in these desperately difficult circumstances they put up such a magnificent fight and stayed in contention right up to the final whistle. For any coach, that last week was a nightmare scenario. Scott Quinnell didn't train all week, Neil Back trained one day, Jonny Wilkinson didn't start training until the Thursday with his injury from the second Test. I could go on and on. Brian O'Driscoll only trained on the Friday before the Test. Rob Henderson had trouble with his knees and didn't train much all week. Will Greenwood dropped out unfit in the middle of the week, and Austin Healey, who was selected on the wing, dropped out on the Saturday morning, leaving us not only without a right wing but with no cover for scrum half. I'm just scratching the surface, but you can understand it was the most depressing week of the tour. However, the guys, despite everything, showed a huge resilience and personal pride in getting up there and trying to do the business, which was a tremendous achievement. To be 23-23 with 20 minutes to go was truly remarkable.

Without trying to look for excuses, the fact is that none of us can remember a tour so crippled by injuries. During the six weeks, you probably lost ten Test players. At the outset, you could never have imagined how bad it would be.

No, you can't ever visualise those things happening. We had a lot of class players who were obviously Test candidates who either never featured in the Test series or featured early and didn't finish the Test series. There was probably over a third of the side I would have chosen who couldn't play in the final Test or the final two Tests, and when you're playing the world champions that's obviously not the ideal situation.

It struck me that the one really disappointing area of the Lions performance was the line out in the second and third Tests. It seemed the ball was thrown to the back in vain far too often. Do you accept the line out cost the Lions dear?

Certainly. We put more time into the line out in training than anything else but it didn't work for us. I guess because the Australians are so good at competing against our ball it destroyed some of our confidence. You have to remember the Wallabies have just about the most competitive line out in world rugby. All three of their main jumpers – John Eales, David Giffin and Justin Harrison – relish the challenge of competing for opposition line-out ball, and they made a point of making it very difficult for us. Obviously we are disappointed, but it wasn't through a lack of work or a lack of thought. We tried to change the line out for the second and third Tests, but it still didn't work. So, yes, it was a disappointing part of the game.

Who actually called the line-out shots? Was it Martin Johnson or Keith Wood or the scrum half?

Keith Wood calls them, but the players have got the opportunity to change that.

What do you think was the one thing you would say cost the Lions the third Test?

As I said in the final press conference, our big chance to win the series was in Melbourne. The intercept try straight after half-time was probably the key factor on the whole tour. It was the defining moment of the tour. If that hadn't occurred, then maybe we would have gone on and won that Test and the series. We scored seven tries each on this tour, so you couldn't get it closer. They probably kicked more goals than we did, they handled the pressures better than we did, and it's understandable I think to some extent when you look at the build-up to the third Test.

You mentioned the goal-kicking. Jonny Wilkinson, who has got a phenomenal percentage for England, in the second and third Tests missed seven kicks out of fourteen, and other players, one or two of the very top players, never hit top form on this tour. You can't legislate for that, can you?

No. The ball we were using in these Tests was a shocking ball in comparison with what we use at home. It's only been used for the Lions Test series so

The end of a long, hard road. Martin Johnson shakes John Eales by the hand after the third Test at Stadium Australia.

I guess it was worth a lot of money to the Australian Rugby Union, but it was a poor ball, and our guys found it difficult to kick properly with it. On the second point, I have to agree that some players we thought would be in the Test team struggled and will be very disappointed with their form on tour.

The most controversial part of the tour featured one or two players who wrote articles for British newspapers, criticising the tour, the coaching and even included personal attacks on Australian players. How upset were you with this?

Well, it's very disappointing. It's disappointing because in my opinion the team comes first and the individuals second, and I think a lot of the players and the management were also very disappointed with what was said, but I don't want to go into details. I'll just leave it at that.

How great is this Australian side? They are the world champions, the Tri-Nations champions, they hold the Bledisloe Cup, the Mandela Cup and they now hold the Tom Richards Cup. Are they the best team in the world?

I don't think there's much doubt about that. The Australians are a very good side because they can handle the pressures on the field and they don't fall apart at line outs as we did, for example. But in saying that, if you had the Australian side touring the UK after 11 months of rugby and 50-odd club and international games it would be a different situation again. That's not taking anything away from them; they are a great side.

The tour postscript reads – Great victory in the first Test, the Lions should have won the second Test and could have won the third. Looking back on the whole trip, has it been one of the great experiences of your rugby life?

Yes. I'll look back on it and think, 'Well, I wouldn't have missed that for anything'. You very seldom get a chance like this; it's very rare and I'm very privileged to have had the opportunity. It's been great to work with some marvellous professional players, coaches and management, but the ultimate objective is to win. That is the way it is these days, and that didn't happen, so that's disappointing.

FROM AN AUSTRALIAN VIEWPOINT
by MICHAEL LYNAGH

The last Test was without doubt the biggest rugby game ever played in Australia. There was an enormous amount at stake and the interest in the game was unprecedented. World Cup finals are huge in this country, but the Wallabies have never played one on home soil. The players realised the importance of this game against the British Lions. It was a once-in-a-career opportunity.

Strange how history repeated itself, with the dominant team in the first Test being the losers of the series at the end of the day – just like in 1989. The third Test was the tensest game of rugby I have ever seen. The build-up was incredible, and it was carried into the Test match, where every moment was stressful. This tension showed in the some of the play, and mistakes were made. This only added to the special nature of the game rather than detracting from it.

For me there were four decisive moments in the game that tilted it the Australians' way. The first came when Justin Harrison stole the first Lions line out of the game. He put this source of ball supply for the Lions under pressure for the rest of the match. The second moment came with 32 minutes remaining. Australia received a kickable penalty. John Eales made the decision to go for a try and kicked to touch. The first attack was driven back by the Lions but not far enough. From the next play the Wallabies managed to put Daniel Herbert over for his second try.

A very short time after scoring this try, Herbert was given a rest on the sideline for a coat-hanger tackle on his opposite number, Brian O'Driscoll. During his ten-minute absence, the Lions failed to score any points. At one stage they had a scrum in the Wallabies' quarter. I counted the overlap they had engineered – it totalled six men to the Wallabies' four defenders. The Lions still didn't manage to score, with O'Driscoll dropping the ball within sight of the line.

The final point that decided this game came minutes from the end. The Lions had a line out five metres from the Wallaby try line. They were six points down and the feeling in the ground, given that the Lions had driven the Wallaby pack from the line outs throughout the game, was that a try was a foregone conclusion. Wilkinson would have a kick from wide out for the series. Justin Harrison, playing in his first Test match, persuaded his more seasoned colleagues that he could win the ball. Captain John Eales, showing great leadership in trusting his men, told him to go for it. Harrison thought that the Lions would go to their banker jumper, Martin Johnson. He guessed correctly, got in front of Johnson and stole the ball. What a moment that was! You could hear the liberation as every Australian in the crowd let out a collective sigh of relief.

This was a true Test match. It tested the combatants, and every one of them gave everything they had. The result was never clear-cut. In fact, as the final whistle blew, the Lions had a chance to win. Had a pass gone in front of the man rather than behind him the result could have been different. That is how close it was. After three games of rugby it came down to the final pass to decide the winner.

The defence in this game was incredible. In the previous two Tests both teams were guilty of leaking in defence. Not in this one. Every contact situation was ferociously contested. It is said that rugby is a contact sport. Wrong. Ballroom dancing is a contact sport; this game was collision sport.

This tour and, ultimately, the result have been magnificent for Australian rugby. The Lions have created unprecedented interest in the game in this country, culminating in the biggest game ever played here. The supporters have been fantastic. It is a pity that some of the more vocal and spoilt players in the touring party couldn't learn a bit from them. They were a happy and very visible bunch. They were well liked throughout the country. Everyone from taxi drivers to restaurant and bar owners welcomed them with open arms. They also forced the Australian Rugby Union to try to compete with the red tide, by issuing gold hats and scarves at the Test matches. It all added up to an extraordinary ambience at the games.

All rugby followers in Australia are already looking forward to seeing the famous red-shirted Lions and their supporters back here again.

Postscript by LAWRENCE DALLAGLIO

After all the glory and excitement of the 1997 Lions tour to South Africa, which will always remain one of the highlights of my whole rugby career, the 2001 tour to Australia was an anticlimax, both for me personally and for the Lions, in that they lost a series they could and probably should have won. A lot has been said and written about the Lions failure in the second and third Tests, and in the final analysis this has been attributed to a desperately unlucky run of injuries and an unexpected inability to win our own ball at the line out.

The injuries we could do nothing about, but Graham Henry lost a lot of top-class players who would have been in serious contention for places in the Test team. Right at the start, Phil Greening dropped out of the tour without taking part in a single game, and another member of the original group of three hookers, Robin McBryde, also left the tour before the Test series got under way.

In the back row there were all sorts of problems which made life really difficult for team selection. I had worked really hard to reach full fitness two weeks before the first Test, and everything seemed to be going well when I survived the midweek match against Australia A in Gosford and then played again on the Saturday against the New South Wales Waratahs. It was shattering for me when my knee gave way in the second half of that match and I realised my Lions tour was over. Watching the first Test from the stand was not what I had hoped for when we landed in Perth three weeks earlier. It is the ultimate ambition of every player in Britain and Ireland to play Test rugby for the Lions, and having done so in South Africa in 1997 I was desperate to do it again in 2001.

The rest of the Lions trip was a very frustrating experience for me, but I was still part of the squad as they prepared for the Brisbane Test, and I was able to share the burning desire in the camp to win that first Test. Apart from the back row, forward selection was pretty straightforward for all three Tests because the front five had virtually no injury problems. Not so the loose forwards. Besides my demise, Neil Back was unavailable for the first Test, Colin Charvis was unavailable for the second and Richard Hill for the third. Scott Quinnell carried knocks in the second and was unable to train on a single occasion between the final whistle in Melbourne and the start of the final Test in Sydney. By half-time in the third Test he had to be replaced. Martin Corry had to play in the unaccustomed role of blind-side flanker in all three Tests.

The backs had even more problems than the back row. Three guys who would have been almost guaranteed a place in the Test team – Dan Luger, Mike Catt and Will Greenwood – were all ruled out of the whole Test series through injury. Rob Howley's rib damage sustained at the end of the second Test ruled him out of the third, and Austin Healey, chosen for Sydney, dropped out on the morning of the game with back problems. When you think that both centres, Brian O'Driscoll and Rob Henderson, were unfit to train for virtually the whole of the final week of the tour, it is a huge testament to the character of the side that they made such a heroic effort in Sydney.

Contrary to many reports which emanated from the tour, I believe that the fact that the Lions stayed in contention right to the final whistle of the final Test was in no small part attributable to the huge workload we put in as a squad in the first three weeks of the trip. I don't accept the criticism that we trained far too hard in the build-up to the first Test and believe a lot of rubbish has been spouted on this subject. This is the modern professional era, and the players are paid to do a professional job. This was always going to be a very difficult and demanding Test series against the best team in the world.

There was no way the Lions were going to overcome them by spending the first three weeks in Australia playing with a bucket and spade on the beach or enjoying 18 holes of golf every day. Hard work had to be done, and every self-respecting professional rugby player on the tour accepted that. To train twice a day early on in the tour was

Danny Grewcock is held aloft by Tom Smith and Phil Vickery as the Lions practise line-out drills ahead of the third Test.

essential to blend the various talents of people from four different countries playing four different styles of rugby. The styles of England, Scotland, Ireland and Wales may not differ a huge amount, but there are nevertheless significant differences.

This had to be a massive challenge for Graham Henry and Andy Robinson, and I supported their approach to training 100 per cent. On a single-nation tour it is quite different. Line-out practice, for example, is simply a continuation of the domestic season. On an England tour we would have the usual two hookers throwing in to the usual line-out jumpers supported by the usual props. A Lions tour is not like that. Keith Wood, the Irish hooker, spent three Tests throwing in to four jumpers – Martin Johnson, Danny Grewcock, Scott Quinnell and Martin Corry – he would never normally throw to. Prop Tom Smith, who played in all three Tests, was supporting these jumpers, with the exception of Martin Johnson, for the very first time.

I have a great deal of respect for both Graham Henry and Andy Robinson, and I strongly believe it is quite wrong to blame them in any way for training the guys too hard early on. Two sessions a day of two hours should be within the compass of every serious professional rugby player, and the coaches tapered off this intensive training before the Test series began in earnest. They laid the foundations in the first three weeks of June for the magnificent victory in the first Test in Brisbane.

One major difference between the 1997 and 2001 tours was the amount of extra time the additional coaches demanded of the players. In Australia we had several specialist coaches, who each demanded their pound of flesh. We had a fitness coach, a kicking coach, a defensive coach and a video analyst coach, and they all wanted time with the players. This became very time-consuming and it meant the players had much less free time than players had had on previous tours.

But that now is surely the nature of the beast. This was also the shortest Lions tour of all time. But Australia, New Zealand and South Africa also embark on equally short, often even shorter, tours off-season to Europe, so we all have to accept that this is the way the game is going.

The fact is that the Lions came very close indeed to toppling the world champions and winning the series, and if it had not been for so many injures I am absolutely certain they would have won at least one of the last two Tests. If that had happened no one would have mentioned the possibility that the squad was overtrained in the first part of the tour.

I firmly believe the two main coaches did a first-class job, and the proof, if proof were needed, can be seen in the statistics from the first seven matches. Two easy wins in Perth and Townsville, where the team played some excellent rugby against fairly moderate opposition, were followed up with a fantastic win over Queensland in Brisbane. You have to remember Queensland reached the semi-finals of the Super-12 competition and the Lions played some stunning rugby to put them to the sword. That was a tremendous victory. My first game sadly marked the Lions' first defeat, when we failed to fire against a competitive Australia A team. This was a setback but not a disaster. Two wins followed before the first Test.

The first two Tests in 1997 produced dramatic victories over South Africa, and I honestly think the win in Brisbane in the first Test of the 2001 tour was every bit as good as the victories in Cape Town and Durban, perhaps even better. The Lions played superbly in the first hour. Curiously enough the Lions failed to score in the final 20 minutes of any of the three Tests, but it certainly didn't matter in Brisbane. The Wallabies finished the match strongly and there's no doubt that served as a warning that they would be there all guns blazing in the second Test in Melbourne!

Having said that, I thought the Lions were outstanding in the first half of the second Test, and it was very flattering to the Wallabies that the Lions only led 11-6 at the interval. We had dominated the whole game in the first 40 minutes and we should have led by 20 points. If we had, we would have gone on to win the Test and the series. Four times in the first half the Lions burst Australia's defence to create four gilt-edged scoring chances. Dafydd James, Scott Quinnell, Martin Johnson and Keith Wood each ripped big holes in the Wallaby cover, and at least two tries should have resulted. Unfortunately we lacked sufficient support on two occasions and took the wrong options on the other two. We had done the hard work but fell down on the simple tasks.

The turning point of the match, and one of the defining moments of the tour, came shortly after half-time. Just as Brian O'Driscoll's try at the start of the second half in Brisbane wrapped up that match for the Lions, so Joe Roff's intercept try turned the second Test Australia's way. For the Lions it was a double disaster. We should have been 20 points up at half-time, but now suddenly two minutes into the second half it was 11-11. The momentum of the match changed. Within a few minutes a Burke penalty and a second Joe Roff try left the Lions trailing 21-11. The world champions started to play with confidence and they squashed the series.

Melbourne was where we should have sewn things up in the first half. A superhuman effort in the third Test against all the odds gave the Lions a final chance, with the scores level at 23-23 with 20 minutes left and Daniel Herbert sin-binned for a dangerous head-high tackle on Brian O'Driscoll. This was the second defining moment of the series. In the ten minutes Herbert was off, the Lions failed to score, apart from the penalty for the dangerous tackle.

The other disaster for the Lions was the line out. We had trouble in Melbourne and even more difficulty in Sydney. Danny Grewcock won virtually every single ball we threw to him, but we hardly threw to him at all in Sydney. We threw long, which is the best attacking ball, but for a variety of reasons we kept failing to win the ball at the back. This cost us the match and the series. Hindsight usually gives 20/20 vision, and in retrospect we would probably have done a lot better throwing to Grewcock and Martin Johnson, although even Martin lost a couple of throws in Sydney – a very rare occurrence.

It was bitterly disappointing to lose such a fantastic series, and it was sad to let down the 25,000 British and Irish fans who flocked to every Test in a blaze of red jerseys to give tremendous support to the team. It made for a great atmosphere, a great occasion and a great Test series. Just a pity about the final result.

Tour Statistics

FRIDAY 8 JUNE 2001 THE WACA, PERTH
Western Australia 10 British & Irish Lions 116

Western Australia: 15 Shannon Apaapa; 14 Mark Gardiner, 13 Aaron Broughton, 12 Hamish Waldin, 11 Brent Becroft; 10 Todd Feather, 9 Mark Fleet; 1 Tim Stevens, 2 Campbell Duff, 3 Adam New; 4 Nathan Hollis, 5 Trefor Thomas (c); 6 Hamish Grace, 8 Anthony Brain, 7 Richard Coney.
Bench: 16 Duncan McRae (21 mins for Feather), 17 Robbie Barugh (51 for Fleet), 18 Matt Harrington, 19 Patricio Noriega (30 for New), 20 Tim Cameron (58 for Coney), 21 Greg Plimmer, 22 Rob Kellam (62 for Duff).
Scorers: *Tries:* Becroft, Barugh.

British & Irish Lions: 15 B. O'Driscoll; 14 B. Cohen, 13 W. Greenwood, 12 M. Taylor, 11 D. Luger; 10 R. O'Gara, 9 R. Howley; 1 D. Morris, 2 K. Wood (c), 3 P. Vickery; 4 D. Grewcock, 5 M. O'Kelly; 6 R. Hill, 8 S. Quinnell, 7 N. Back.
Bench: 16 I. Balshaw (55 mins for Greenwood), 17 R. Henderson (62 for Cohen), 18 A. Healey (54-77 for Howley; 77 for Balshaw), 19 S. Taylor (40 for Hill), 20 J. Davidson (41-46 for Quinnell), 21 J. Leonard (58 for Vickery), 22 R. McBryde (71 for Wood).
Scorers: *Tries:* Luger(3), Quinnell(3), Back(2), Howley(2), Balshaw(2), Greenwood, Grewcock, M. Taylor, Healey, S. Taylor, O'Driscoll. *Conversions:* O'Gara(13).

Referee: Wayne Erickson.
Attendance: 20,695.

SNIPPETS
• The Lions biggest win, beating the 97-0 against South-West Districts at Mossel Bay, South Africa, 29 May 1974.
• The 18 tries scored broke the Lions record for tries in a match, surpassing the 16 achieved three times before – v Western Australia in 1930, Eastern Canada in 1959 and South-West Districts in 1974.
• Ronan O'Gara's 26 points on Lions debut broke Phil Bennett's previous mark on Lions debut – 23 points v Western Transvaal in 1974.

TUESDAY, 12 JUNE, 2001 DAIRY FARMERS STADIUM, TOWNSVILLE
Queensland President's XV 6 British & Irish Lions 83

Queensland President's XV: 15 Nathan Williams; 14 David McCallum, 13 Junior Pelesasa, 12 Jason Ramsamy, 11 Scott Barton; 10 Shane Drahm, 9 Ben Wakely; 1 Rick Tyrrell, 2 Sean Hardman (c), 3 Fletcher Dyson; 4 Mike Mitchell, 5 Rudi Vedelago; 6 Tom McVerry, 8 John Roe, 7 Scott Fava.
Bench: 16 Sean Barry (74 mins for Wakely), 17 Andrew Scotney (57 for Drahm), 18 Michael Tabrett (18-68 for Williams), 19 David Duley, 20 Andrew Farley (65 for Vedelago), 21 Simon Kerr (8 for Dyson), 22 Tim Tavalea (65 for Hardman).
Scorers: *Penalties:* Drahm(2).

British & Irish Lions: 15 M. Perry; 14 D. James, 13 W. Greenwood, 12 R. Henderson, 11 J. Robinson; 10 N. Jenkins, 9 M. Dawson; 1 T. Smith, 2 R. McBryde, 3 D. Young (c); 4 J. Davidson, 5 S. Murray; 6 C. Charvis, 8 M. Corry, 7 M. Williams.
Bench: 16 A. Healey (65 mins for Jenkins), 17 M. Taylor (65 for Greenwood), 18 D. Luger, 19 R. Hill, 20 M. O'Kelly (67 for Davidson), 21 J. Leonard (59 for Smith), 22 G. Bulloch (8 for McBryde).
Scorers: *Tries:* Robinson(5), Henderson(3), Charvis(2), Young, penalty try, O'Kelly. *Conversions:* Jenkins(5), Perry(4).

Referee: George Ayoub.
Attendance: 19,000.

SNIPPETS
• Jason Robinson became the first Lion to score five tries on debut and the sixth – the first since Andy Irvine against King Country/Wanganui in 1977 – to score five or more tries in a match.
• The Lions scored 73 points in the second half, beating their previous best of 60 v South-West Districts in 1974.
• The Lions were awarded only their fifth penalty try – the last two were on the tour of New Zealand in 1993.
• Dai Young skippered the Lions for the first time.

Stan James Telebetting keeps you both in touch and in play...

WE NEVER CLOSE! **24** HR BETTING

ANYTIME, ANY PLACE, ANYWHERE!

SATURDAY 16 JUNE 2001 BALLYMORE, BRISBANE
Queensland Reds **8** British & Irish Lions **42**

Queensland Reds: 15 Michael Tabrett; 14 Junior Pelesasa, 13 Daniel Herbert (c), 12 Steve Kefu, 11 David McCallum; 10 Elton Flatley, 9 Sam Cordingley; 1 Nic Stiles, 2 Michael Foley, 3 Glenn Panoho; 4 Nathan Sharpe, 5 Mark Connors; 6 Matt Cockbain, 8 Toutai Kefu, 7 David Croft.
Bench: 16 Ben Wakely (82 mins for Cordingley), 17 Andrew Scotney (40 for Flatley), 18 Jason Ramsamy (52 for S. Kefu), 19 John Roe (36-38 for T. Kefu; 80 for Cockbain), 20 Mike Mitchell (68 for Sharpe), 21 Simon Kerr (65 for Stiles), 22 Sean Hardman (63 for Foley).
Scorers: *Try:* Cordingley. *Penalty:* Flatley.

British & Irish Lions: 15 I. Balshaw; 14 D. James, 13 B. O'Driscoll, 12 R. Henderson, 11 D. Luger; 10 J. Wilkinson, 9 R. Howley; 1 T. Smith, 2 K. Wood, 3 P. Vickery; 4 M. Johnson (c), 5 D. Grewcock; 6 R. Hill, 8 M. Corry, 7 N. Back.
Bench: 16 A. Healey, 17 G. Bulloch, 18 S. Murray (82 mins for Johnson), 19 C. Charvis (76 for Back), 20 M. Dawson (47 for Howley), 21 J. Leonard, 22 J. Robinson (61 for O'Driscoll).
Scorers: *Tries:* Luger, Henderson, James, Hill, O'Driscoll. *Conversions:* Wilkinson(4). *Penalties:* Wilkinson(3).

Referee: Stuart Dickinson.
Attendance: 18,337.

SNIPPETS

• The match was the first occasion since the victory over Western Australia in 1989 that all four starting Lions three-quarters have scored tries (it also happened against Queensland in 1966).
• Jonny Wilkinson missed with his first kick at goal (a conversion) but thereafter landed seven from seven, including the first three penalty goals attempted by the Lions on the 2001 tour.
• The Lions have now won four of the five matches they have played at Ballymore. Their only loss was on their first visit in 1971 also against Queensland.

TUESDAY 19 JUNE 2001 NORTHPOWER STADIUM, GOSFORD
Australia A **28** British & Irish Lions **25**

Australia A: 15 Richard Graham; 14 Mark Batholomeusz, 13 Scott Staniforth, 12 Nathan Grey, 11 Graeme Bond; 10 Manuel Edmonds, 9 Chris Whitaker; 1 Cameron Blades, 2 Brendan Cannon, 3 Rod Moore; 4 Tom Bowman, 5 Justin Harrison; 6 David Lyons, 8 Jim Williams, 7 Phil Waugh (c).
Bench: 16 Tom Murphy (74 mins for Cannon), 17 Patricio Noriega (62 for Blades), 18 Jono West (61 for Bowman), 19 Sam Payne (59 for Whitaker), 20 Julian Huxley, 21 Peter Ryan (41-46 for Williams; 70 for Williams), 22 James Holbeck (25 for Graham).
Scorers: *Try:* Staniforth. *Conversion:* Edmonds. *Penalties:* Edmonds(7).

British & Irish Lions: 15 M. Perry; 14 B. Cohen, 13 W. Greenwood, 12 M. Catt, 11 J. Robinson; 10 N. Jenkins, 9 A. Healey; 1 J. Leonard, 2 R. McBryde, 3 D. Young (c); 4 S. Murray, 5 M. O'Kelly; 6 L. Dallaglio, 8 S. Quinnell, 7 M. Williams.
Bench: 16 D. Morris (69 mins for Young), 17 G. Bulloch (53 for McBryde), 18 J. Davidson (53 for O'Kelly), 19 C. Charvis (34-43 for Quinnell), 20 M. Dawson (59 for Jenkins), 21 R. O'Gara, 22 M. Taylor (45 for Catt).
Yellow card: 73-84 mins Dallaglio.
Scorers: *Tries:* Taylor, Perry, Robinson. *Conversions:* Dawson(2). *Penalties:* Jenkins(2).

Referee: Paul Honiss.
Attendance: 17,026

SNIPPETS

• The Lions conceded seven successful penalty goal attempts for the first time. All kicks were slotted by Manny Edmonds. Grant Fox for Auckland against the Lions in June 1993 held the previous record with six.
• During the second half, Lawrence Dallaglio became the first Lions player ever to be sin-binned.
• Mike Catt and Lawrence Dallaglio made their tour debuts. Catt's game lasted only into first-half injury time when a calf injury saw his replacement by Mark Taylor.

SATURDAY 23 JUNE 2001 SYDNEY FOOTBALL STADIUM
NSW Waratahs **24** British & Irish Lions **41**

New South Wales Waratahs: 15 Duncan McRae; 14 Francis Cullimore, 13 Luke Inman, 12 Sam Harris, 11 Sikeli Qau Qau; 10 Manuel Edmonds, 9 Sam Payne; 1 Cameron Blades, 2 Brendan Cannon, 3 Rod Moore; 4 Jono West, 5 Tom Bowman; 6 Stu Pinkerton (81-85 for West), 8 Fili Finau, 7 Phil Waugh (c).
Bench: 16 Patricio Noriega (61-63 for Besseling; 68 for Moore), 17 Jeff Mutton (79 for Harris), 18 Lee Green (61-63 for Finau; 79 for Blades), 19 Peter Besseling (ht for Bowman), 20 Drew Hickey (66 for Finau), 21 Richard Tombs (71 for Inman), 22 Ed Carter (72 for Pinkerton).
Red card: 55 mins McRae.
Yellow cards: 58-71 mins Blades and Cannon.
Scorers: *Tries:* Pinkerton, Cullimore, Harris, Edmonds. *Conversions:* Edmonds(2).

British & Irish Lions: 15 I. Balshaw; 14 D. James, 13 B. O'Driscoll, 12 W. Greenwood, 11 J. Robinson; 10 J. Wilkinson, 9 M. Dawson; 1 D. Morris, 2 K. Wood, 3 P. Vickery; 4 M. Johnson (c), 5 D. Grewcock; 6 L. Dallaglio, 8 S. Quinnell, 7 N. Back.
Bench: 16 T. Smith (61-71 mins for Quinnell; 71 for Vickery), 17 R. McBryde (85 for Wood), 18 M. Corry, 19 R. Hill (78 for Back), 20 A. Healey (81 for Wilkinson), 21 R. O'Gara (24 for Greenwood), 22 M. Perry (55 for O'Gara).
Yellow cards: 58-71 mins Vickery and Grewcock.
Scorers: *Tries:* Robinson(2), O'Driscoll, Wilkinson, James. *Conversions:* Wilkinson(4), Dawson. *Penalties:* Wilkinson(2).

Referee: Scott Young.
Attendance: 40,128.

SNIPPETS
• Duncan McRae became only the second opponent ever to be sent off against the Lions; the first such dismissal was also in Australia, when W. G. Cobb was sent off for Newcastle on 27 July 1899.
• Jason Robinson and Brian O'Driscoll joined a select band of only a dozen other Lions who scored tries in their first three starts for the side; the last was Trevor Ringland in 1983.

TUESDAY 26 JUNE 2001 COFFS HARBOUR
NSW Country Cockatoos **3** British & Irish Lions **46**

New South Wales Country Cockatoos: 15 Nathan Croft; 14 Vuli Tailasa, 13 Ryan MacDougal, 12 Kieran Shepherd, 11 Warwick Crosby; 10 Chris Doyle, 9 Rod Petty; 1 Angus Baldwin, 2 James McCormack, 3 Matt Bowman; 4 David Lubans, 5 Ben Wright; 6 Brent Dale, 8 Bernie Klasen, 7 Craig Taylor.
Bench: 16 Matt Brown (66 for Shepherd), 17 Matt Ellis (70 for Doyle), 18 David Banovich (63 for MacDougal), 19 Darel Thomas (70 for Baldwin), 20 John Vaalotu (66 for McCormack), 21 Gordon Refshauge (60 for Wright), 22 Darren Dimmock (60 for Taylor).
Scorer: *Penalty:* Croft.

British & Irish Lions: 15 I. Balshaw; 14 B. Cohen, 13 M. Taylor, 12 S. Gibbs, 11 T. Howe; 10 N. Jenkins, 9 A. Healey; 1 J. Leonard, 2 G. Bulloch, 3 D. Young (c); 4 J. Davidson, 5 M. O'Kelly; 6 C. Charvis, 8 M. Corry, 7 M. Williams.
Bench: 16 D. Morris (56-61 mins for Leonard; 62 for Leonard), 17 D. West, 18 S. Murray (71 for O'Kelly), 19 D. Wallace (57 for Corry), 20 M. Dawson, 21 R. O'Gara (8-16 for Gibbs), 22 M. Perry.
Scorers: *Tries:* Cohen(2), Charvis, Gibbs, Healey, Young. *Conversions:* Jenkins(5). *Penalties:* Jenkins(2).

Referee: Greg Hinton.
Attendance: 9,972.

SNIPPETS
• Three tour replacements – Scott Gibbs, Tyrone Howe and Gordon Bulloch – made their first starts of the trip. Another replacement, David Wallace, also made his bow as a replacement.
• By the end of the game the Lions had racked up 50 tries in the six tour matches to date.
• This was the first major rugby match to be played at the Wallabies training camp at Coffs Harbour.
• The New South Wales Country XV have been playing touring teams since 1903 but have managed just one victory – in 1975 they beat an England XV 14-13 at Goulburn.

SATURDAY 30 JUNE 2001 THE GABBA, BRISBANE
Australia **13** British & Irish Lions **29**

Australia: 15 Chris Latham; 14 Andrew Walker, 13 Daniel Herbert, 12 Nathan Grey, 11 Joe Roff; 10 Stephen Larkham, 9 George Gregan; 1 Nick Stiles, 2 Jeremy Paul, 3 Glenn Panoho; 4 David Giffin, 5 John Eales (c); 6 Owen Finegan, 8 Toutai Kefu, 7 George Smith.
Bench: 16 Michael Foley (56 mins for Paul), 17 Ben Darwin (69 for Panoho), 18 Matt Cockbain (73 for Eales), 19 David Lyons (83 for Finegan), 20 Chris Whitaker, 21 Elton Flatley (56 for Larkham), 22 Matt Burke (40 for Latham).
Scorers: *Tries:* Walker, Grey. *Penalty:* Walker.

British & Irish Lions: 15 M. Perry; 14 D. James, 13 B. O'Driscoll, 12 R. Henderson, 11 J. Robinson; 10 J. Wilkinson, 9 R. Howley; 1 T. Smith, 2 K. Wood, 3 P. Vickery; 4 M. Johnson (c), 5 D. Grewcock; 6 M. Corry, 8 S. Quinnell, 7 R. Hill.
Bench: 16 J. Leonard (83 mins for Smith), 17 G. Bulloch (75-82 for Wood), 18 C. Charvis (71 for Quinnell), 19 M. Williams, 20 M. Dawson, 21 A. Healey, 22 I. Balshaw (40 for Perry).
Yellow cards: 70-82 mins Corry; 85 Vickery.
Scorers: *Tries:* Robinson, James, O'Driscoll, Quinnell. *Conversions:* Wilkinson(3). *Penalty:* Wilkinson.

Referee: Andre Watson.
Attendance: 37,460

SNIPPETS
• The Lions have recorded just one higher score against the Wallabies, 31-0 in 1966.
• Brian O'Driscoll became the fifth Lion to score tries on his first four appearances after Paul Clauss in South Africa in 1891, John Young in Australia & New Zealand (1959), Mike Weston in Southern Africa (1962) and John Bevan in Australia & New Zealand (1971). Bevan went on to score (four times) on his fifth appearance.
• Jason Robinson became the eighth player since the war to play in a Lions Test before starting a Test for his home country, following Dickie Jeeps in 1955, Bill Patterson (1959), Delme Thomas (1966), Derek Quinnell (1971), and Gareth Evans, Elgan Rees and Brynmor Williams (1977).

TUESDAY 3 JULY 2001 BRUCE STADIUM, CANBERRA
ACT Brumbies **28** British & Irish Lions **30**

Australian Capital Territory Brumbies: 15 Mark Bartholomeusz; 14 Damien McInally, 13 James Holbeck, 12 Graeme Bond, 11 Willie Gordon; 10 Pat Howard, 9 Travis Hall; 1 Angus Scott, 2 Adam Freier, 3 Matt Weaver; 4 Justin Harrison, 5 Daniel Vickerman; 6 Peter Ryan, Jim Williams (c), 7 Des Tuilavi.
Bench: 16 David Palavi, 17 Damien Drew, 18 David Pusey (47 mins for Vickerman), 19 Radike Samo (54 for Williams), 20 Cameron Pither (78 for Gordon), 21 Julian Huxley (87 for Holbeck), 22 Matt Henjak.
Yellow card: 64-76 mins Ryan.
Scorers: *Tries:* Bartholomeusz, Gordon, Tuilavi. *Conversions:* Hall(2). *Penalties:* Hall(3).

British & Irish Lions: 15 I. Balshaw; 14 B. Cohen, 13 M. Taylor, 12 S. Gibbs, 11 A. Healey; 10 R. O'Gara, 9 M. Dawson; 1 D. Morris, 2 D. West, 3 D. Young (c); 4 J. Davidson, 5 S. Murray; 6 D. Wallace, 8 M. Corry, 7 M. Williams.
Bench: 16 J. Leonard (78 mins for Young), 17 G. Bulloch, 18 M. Johnson, 19 M. O'Kelly, 20 N. Jenkins, 21 D. James (18-21 for Taylor; 74-75 for Healey), 22 T. Howe.
Yellow card: 62-74 mins Balshaw.
Scorers: *Tries:* Healey(2), Wallace. *Conversions:* Dawson(3). *Penalties:* Dawson(3).

Referee: Peter Marshall.
Attendance: 20,093.

SNIPPETS
• In the match against the Brumbies, at 33 years of age, Dorian West became the third oldest Lions debutant of all time, after 36-year-old Tony Faulkner in New Zealand in 1977 and 34-year-old Stanley Hodgson in Rhodesia in 1962.
• Super-12 champions, the ACT Brumbies, were handed only their second defeat at Bruce Stadium in the last two seasons.
• The Lions did not lead this match at any stage until Matt Dawson's 89th-minute conversion of Austin Healey's try.

Tour Statistics

SATURDAY 7 JULY 2001 COLONIAL STADIUM, MELBOURNE
Australia 35 British & Irish Lions 14

Australia: 15 Matt Burke; 14 Andrew Walker, 13 Daniel Herbert, 12 Nathan Grey, 11 Joe Roff; 10 Stephen Larkham, 9 George Gregan; 1 Nic Stiles, 2 Michael Foley, 3 Rod Moore; 4 David Giffin, 5 John Eales (c); 6 Owen Finegan, 8 Toutai Kefu, 7 George Smith.
Bench: 16 Brendan Cannon (89 mins for Foley), 17 Ben Darwin, 18 Matt Cockbain (42-ht for Giffin; 71 for Giffin), 19 David Lyons, 20 Chris Whitaker, 21 Elton Flatley (82 for Larkham), 22 Chris Latham (46 for Walker).
Scorers: Tries: Roff(2), Burke. *Conversion:* Burke. *Penalties:* Burke(6).

British & Irish Lions: 15 M. Perry; 14 D. James, 13 B. O'Driscoll, 12 R. Henderson, 11 J. Robinson; 10 J. Wilkinson, 9 R. Howley; 1 T. Smith, 2 K. Wood, 3 P. Vickery; 4 M. Johnson (c), 5 D. Grewcock; 6 N. Back, 8 S. Quinnell, 7 R. Hill.
Bench: 16 J. Leonard (65 mins for Vickery), 17 D. West, 18 M. Corry (37-39 for Hill; 40 for Hill), 19 M. Williams, 20 M. Dawson (85 for Howley), 21 N. Jenkins (76 for Wilkinson), 22 I. Balshaw (52 for Perry).
Scorers: Try: Back. *Penalties:* Wilkinson(3).

Referee: Jonathan Kaplan.
Attendance: 56,605

SNIPPETS
• The 35 points scored by the Wallabies is their highest in a Test against the Lions and the second best by any team in a Test against the Lions behind New Zealand's 38 in the 38-6 victory at Eden Park in 1983.
• It was the Wallabies' second biggest turnaround; they won by 21 points after trailing by five at half-time. The only bigger turnaround was at Melbourne in 2000 when they trailed the Springboks by six (17-23) at the break and also won by 21 points, 44-23.
• Matt Burke's 25 points were the most for any player in a Test against the Lions, surpassing the previous mark of 18 by All Blacks Don Clarke (1959) and Allan Hewson (1983). Burke's six penalty goals also tied Clarke's record for the most penalty goals converted in a Lions Test.
• Australia preserved their record of not losing two successive home Tests since the Lions last toured in 1989.

SATURDAY 14 JUL 2001 STADIUM AUSTRALIA, SYDNEY
Australia 29 British & Irish Lions 23

Australia: 15 Matt Burke; 14 Andrew Walker, 13 Daniel Herbert, 12 Nathan Grey, 11 Joe Roff; 10 Elton Flatley, 9 George Gregan; 1 Nic Stiles, 2 Michael Foley, 3 Rod Moore; 4 Justin Harrison, 5 John Eales (c); 6 Owen Finegan, 8 Toutai Kefu, 7 George Smith.
Bench: 16 Brendan Cannon, 17 Ben Darwin, 18 Matt Cockbain (75 mins for Finegan), 19 David Lyons, 20 Chris Whitaker, 21 James Holbeck (79 for Grey), 22 Chris Latham.
Yellow card: 51-64 mins Herbert
Scorers: Tries: Herbert(2). *Conversions:* Burke(2). *Penalties:* Burke(5).

British & Irish Lions: 15 M. Perry; 14 D. James, 13 B. O'Driscoll, 12 R. Henderson, 11 J. Robinson; 10 J. Wilkinson, 9 M. Dawson; 1 T. Smith, 2 K. Wood, 3 P. Vickery; 4 M. Johnson (c), 5 D. Grewcock; 6 N. Back, 8 S. Quinnell, 7 M. Corry.
Bench: 16 D. Morris (74 mins for Smith), 17 D. West, 18 C. Charvis (ht for Quinnell), 19 M. Williams, 20 R. O'Gara, 21 A. Nicol, 22 I. Balshaw (73 for James).
Scorers: Tries: Robinson, Wilkinson. *Conversions:* Wilkinson(2). *Penalties:* Wilkinson(3).

Referee: Paddy O'Brien.
Attendance: 84,188

SNIPPETS
• Tour guide Andy Nicol found his way onto the bench after injury decimated the Lions scrum half ranks. In the end he did not add to his total of three minutes previous Lions experience, gained as a replacement against Taranaki on the 1993 New Zealand tour.
• Jonny Wilkinson's 18 points in the match equalled the Lions record for a Test match – jointly held by Tony Ward in South Africa in 1980 and by Gavin Hastings in New Zealand in 1993.

Tour statistics were compiled by Stuart Farmer Media Services Limited – Official 2001 Lions Statisticians.

Tour Summary

All matches
Played 10, Won 7, Lost 3, For 449, Against 184.

Test matches
Played 3, Won 1, Lost 2, For 66, Against 77.

SQUAD TOTALS

Name	Ctry	Club	App	Try	Pts	App	Try	Pts
			ALL			*TESTS*		
N. Back	E	Leicester	5	3	15	2	1	5
I. Balshaw	E	Bath	4+4	2	10	0+3	-	-
G. Bulloch	S	Glasgow	1+3	-	-	0+1	-	-
M. Catt	E	Bath	1	-	-	-	-	-
C. Charvis	W	Swansea	2+4	3	15	0+2	-	-
B. Cohen	E	N'pton	4	2	10	-	-	-
M. Corry	E	Leicester	6+1	-	-	2+1	-	-
L. Dallaglio	E	Wasps	2	-	-	-	-	-
J. Davidson	I	Castres	3+2	-	-	-	-	-
M. Dawson	E	N'pton	4+3	-	21	1+1	-	-
S. Gibbs	W	Swansea	2	1	5	-	-	-
P. Greening	E	Wasps	-	-	-	-	-	-
W. Greenwood	E	H'quins	4	1	5	-	-	-
D. Grewcock	E	Saracens	6	1	5	3	-	-
A. Healey	E	Leicester	3+3	4	20	-	-	-
R. Henderson	I	Wasps	5+1	4	20	3	-	-
R. Hill	E	Saracens	4+1	1	5	2	-	-
T. Howe	I	Ballymena	1	-	-	-	-	-
R. Howley	W	Cardiff	4	2	10	2	-	-
D. James	W	Llanelli	6+1	3	15	3	1	5
N. Jenkins	W	Cardiff	3+1	-	32	0+1	-	-
M. Johnson	E	Leicester	5	-	-	3	-	-
J. Leonard	E	H'quins	2+5	-	-	0+2	-	-
D. Luger	E	H'quins	2	4	20	-	-	-
R. McBryde	W	Llanelli	2+2	-	-	-	-	-
D. Morris	W	Swansea	3+3	-	-	0+1	-	-
S. Murray	S	Saracens	3+2	-	-	-	-	-
A. Nicol	S	Glasgow	-	-	-	-	-	-
B. O'Driscoll	I	B'rock C	6	4	20	3	1	5
R. O'Gara	I	Cork Const	2+2	-	26	-	-	-
M. O'Kelly	I	St Mary's C	3+1	1	5	-	-	-
M. Perry	E	Bath	5+1	1	13	3	-	-
S. Quinnell	W	Llanelli	6	4	20	3	1	5
J. Robinson	E	Sale	6+1	10	50	3	2	10
T. Smith	S	Brive	5+1	-	-	3	-	-
M. Taylor	W	Swansea	3+2	2	10	-	-	-
S. Taylor	S	Edinburgh	0+1	1	5	-	-	-
P. Vickery	E	Gloucester	6	-	-	3	-	-
D. Wallace	I	Garryowen	1+1	1	5	-	-	-
D. West	E	Leicester	1	-	-	-	-	-
J. Wilkinson	E	Newcastle	5	2	72	3	1	36
M. Williams	W	Cardiff	4	-	-	-	-	-
K. Wood	I	H'quins	6	-	-	3	-	-
D. Young	W	Cardiff	4	2	10	-	-	-
Penalty Tries			-	1	5	-	-	-

PLACE KICKING

		ALL			*TESTS*	
Kicker	Atts	Goals	Rate	Atts	Goals	Rate
M. Dawson	14	9	64.3%	-	-	-
N. Jenkins	19	14	73.7%	-	-	-
R. O'Gara	18	13	72.2%	-	-	-
M. Perry	4	4	100.0%	-	-	-
J. Wilkinson	35	25	71.4%	21	12	57.1%
LIONS	90	65	72.2%	21	12	57.1%
OPPONENTS	57	34	59.6%	23	15	65.2%

SNIPPETS

• Will Greenwood emulated Bob Hiller (1968 and 1971), and Sandy Carmichael (1971 and 1974) by being in the original Lions squad selection and going through two tours without playing in a Test match.

• Matt Burke broke the record for penalty goals in series against the Lions, his 11 surpassing the previous mark of nine set by All Blacks Don Clarke and Allan Hewson.

• For the second time in a row, Australia won a three-Test home series after losing the opening Test, having achieved the same against South Africa in 1993.

• The Lions failed to score a point in the final quarter of any of the three Test matches; the Wallabies scored 30 points in the same periods, including three tries.

• For only the second time in their 25 Test series, the Lions lost a series after they had won the opening Test. The previous occurrence was in New Zealand in 1930, when they won the first Test and lost the next three.

• George Gregan made only seven handling errors in 453 touches during the entire series – four passing errors, two lost in contact, one knock-on from a pick-up.

• Joe Roff made the most metres in the Tests with ball in hand, his 250 metres gained from 19 ball carries and over 60 metres ahead of his closest rival – Scott Quinnell. Third was Brian O'Driscoll with 183 metres. Wallaby centres Dan Herbert and Nathan Grey made 170 metres each for equal fourth on the list.

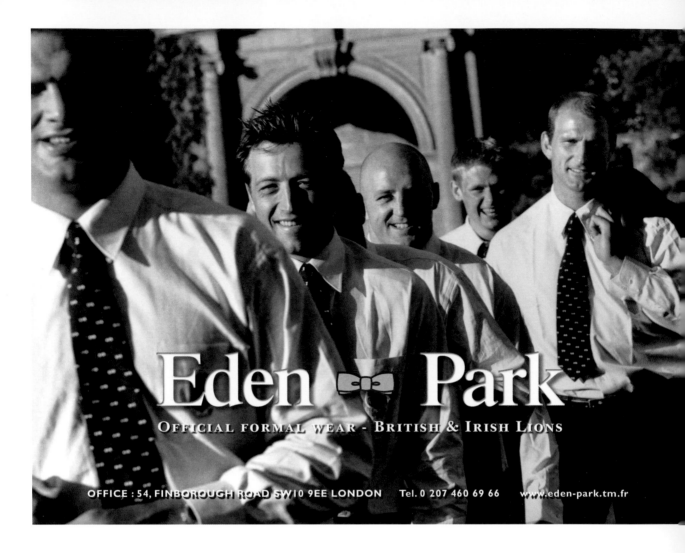

Eden · Park

OFFICIAL FORMAL WEAR - BRITISH & IRISH LIONS

OFFICE : 54, FINBOROUGH ROAD SW10 9EE LONDON   Tel. 0 207 460 69 66   www.eden-park.tm.fr

AND A FINAL THANKS TO

SKYNET
WORLDWIDE EXPRESS

FOR THEIR GENEROUS CONTRIBUTION
TO THIS BOOK AND ALSO FOR THEIR
CO-SPONSORSHIP OF THE DINNER TO
MARK ITS PUBLICATION

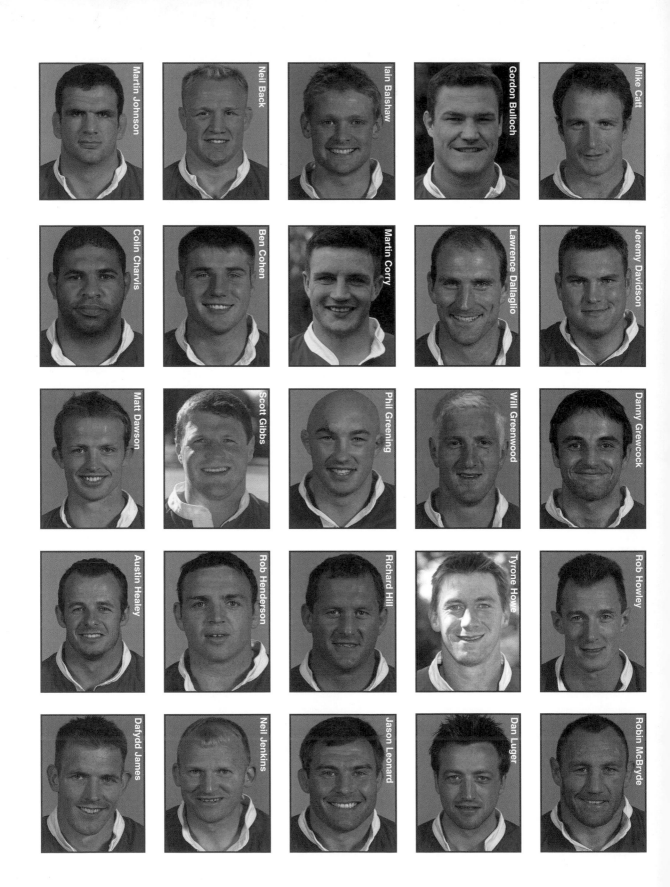